THE MARKS OF HOPE
WHERE THE SPIRIT IS MOVING
IN A WOUNDED CHURCH

Where the Spirit is Moving
in a Wounded Church

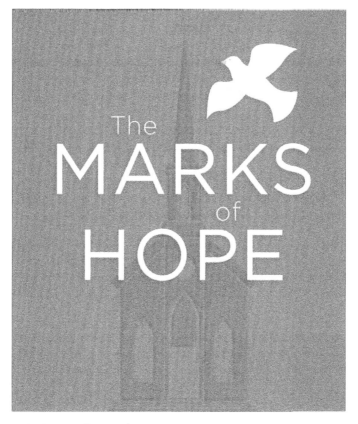

The
MARKS
of
HOPE

Matt Rawle   Juan Huertas
Katie McKay Simpson

Abingdon Press / Nashville

THE MARKS OF HOPE
WHERE THE SPIRIT IS MOVING IN A WOUNDED CHURCH

Copyright © 2018 Abingdon Press
All rights reserved.

This book is printed on elemental chlorine-free paper.
Library of Congress Cataloging-in-Publication has been requested.

978-1-5018-5933-5

18 19 20 21 22 23 24 25 26 27 — 10 9 8 7 6 5 4 3 2 1
MANUFACTURED IN THE UNITED STATES OF AMERICA

CONTENTS

Introduction 7

1. A Story of Hope 13

2. Partnerships with Purpose 29

3. The Language of Justice 51

4. The (Digital) World Is My Parish 75

5. Together We Rise 91

6. Our Mission 115

Notes 137

INTRODUCTION

Matt Rawle

How many times do you think that "hope" is mentioned in the Gospels? You might be surprised that Jesus mentions hope only once (Luke 6:34). Of course, Jesus' ministry was very much about hope—the hope of everlasting life (John 14), the hope of forgiveness (Matthew 6:9-15), the hope that the blind will see, the hungry will be filled, and the mournful comforted (Matthew 5). We light the candle of hope during Advent, we put hope in our church mission statements, we read at weddings that "faith, hope, and love abide, these three; but the greatest of these is love" (1 Corinthians 13:13 ESV). So why does the church proclaim a word that Jesus rarely ever said?

Sometimes when we think about hope we think of an emotion, like a feeling of peace when things aren't going well or a painting of a sunrise with "It's always darkest before the dawn," written underneath. Hopeful words can sound empty. At worst, offering a hopeful word when someone isn't ready to hear them is like pouring salt on a wound rather than a healing touch. Paul writes in Romans 5 that "suffering produces endurance, and endurance produces character, and character produces hope, and hope does not disappoint us" (vv. 3-5 NRSV). Hope goes beyond a feeling or a helpful saying. Hope is a destination that sometimes takes a lifetime to find.

Hope, Faith, and Love

Every year in my church the Adult Council for Youth Ministry (ACYM) gathers in August to decide the destination for our Youth Spring Break Mission Trip. We often choose three destinations and then weigh the pros and cons of each. One location has great need, but travel expenses make it a difficult choice. Another location is closer, but there's not much to do. Another location offers great housing with a day of rafting on the way back. In a way, hope is where you're going. You consider where you are, and hope is where you want to be.

Hope needs help, which is why Paul talks about hope, faith, and love abiding together. Hope has no moral value in and of itself. I can hope that my friend finds healing, or I can hope that my friend never gets well. I can hope that we will find peace, or I can hope that my enemy burns in a blaze of fire and fury. Hope is where you're going, and faith is trusting that where you're going is where you need to be. We can weigh and measure the pros and cons of a mission trip location, but at the end of the day, we have to trust that where we are going is where God is calling us to be.

If hope is where you're going, and faith is trusting that the destination is where you need to be, love is how you get there. Let's say that we decide that Houston is the location of our mission trip, and we trust that God is calling us there. Love is what we call the plan for how many vehicles we need, how many supplies to bring, and where we need to stop along the way. In other words, love is how we get to hope.

Finding Hope in The UMC

So what does it mean to find hope in The United Methodist Church today? To be honest, I don't have much of an answer to what the future global structure of The UMC needs to be. What I do know is that every day I'm charged with loving, serving, challenging, and leading the folks who have found a home in my local church and those who don't yet know God's amazing grace in Jesus Christ. You will find lots of different perspectives in the Fautlines series that will surely foster deep and meaningful conversation as The UMC meanders through the wilderness of tension and division. In *The Marks of Hope*, our perspective comes from being knee-deep in ministry in a local church not of one mind. We teach, preach, counsel, and plan in the midst of good Christian women and men who do not agree, and yet our churches are growing with new disciples, fostering relationships with the poor and neglected, cultivating a place of trust for holy conversations, and creating an environment where we do our best to do justice, love kindness, and walk humbly with God (Micah 6:8).

With a wide-angle lens United Methodist headlines contains words like, *division, death tsunami,* and *WCA vs. RMN.* Amazingly, people keep showing up to worship, small groups, and disaster relief missions. Our people are certainly engaged in the debate, and they have definitive ideas of who God is calling them to be. We three pastors are members of the General Conference delegation of our conference, so we are keenly aware of big-picture Methodism, but something miraculous happens when you shake a hand at the sanctuary doors, sit next to a brother in a covenant group, and pick up a hammer with a sister at a work site. Our commitment to doing the work of building God's kingdom in the person of Jesus seems to supersede commissions, conferences, and judicial rulings. Of course, church would be perfect if it weren't for all the people in it, but when we trade our wide-angle for a zoom lens, these fissures and cracks are held together by real people in a real community trying to cultivate the mustard seed of faith God has graciously offered.

Maybe this is where we find our hope in The United Methodist Church? It's like the time our mission committee debated on whether we should be dedicated to local or global mission. Maybe you've had a similar discussion? We debated cost, effectiveness, and calling. Like the prodigal son who "came to himself," we realized that all mission is local, but it's not always here. All of our churches are local. They just aren't in the same place. This book isn't about structure, local options, contextual disciplines, or commission reports; rather, we want to share the hope we already see in the day-to-day comings and goings of the people called United Methodists.

Story, justice, social entrepreneurship, technology, mission, and leadership are where we see hope in The UMC today and where we know we will see it tomorrow. Regardless of how we categorize our work moving forward, we will still have a story to tell. Justice will continue to be the heartbeat of our prophetic witness. Our partnerships with local businesses and nonprofits will extend our understanding of what it means to follow Christ. Technology advances how we communicate and connect people to Christ and each other. Mission will always keep our idle hands busy with God's work. Cultivating seeds in the heart of those God is calling to serve the church will keep God's movement vibrant for generations.

We can say with great conviction that conflict takes advantage of the space between us. The further apart we are, the easier conflict can find room to cause havoc. Our culture has grown accustomed to smearing our neighbor with our computer keys, but it is much more difficult to slander the person sharing a cup of coffee with us. *The Marks of Hope* is our offering of six ways we might hold one another close with mutual love and accountability. Hope is our destination, faith is trusting in that destination, and love is how we get there.

Chapter One
A STORY OF HOPE

Matt Rawle

Christians find their character by becoming a character in God's story.

—*Sam Wells,* Improvisation:
The Drama of Christian Ethics

It seems that everything around us has a beginning, middle, and end. It's hard not to think of life as the story that happens between "Once upon a time," and "They lived happily ever after." Scripture is, on the whole, God's story from "In the beginning," to "Amen," and our role in God's story is found somewhere in between. When we think about God's story it's important to recognize that this story neither begins nor ends with us, though in the dash between birth and death there are countless beginnings and endings.

A story is an account of what happens (and sometimes what doesn't). The stories we remember usually focus on triumph and perseverance, someone or something that defies the odds and finds victory. Thankfully, we don't have to look very far to find the only story that ultimately matters. Jesus' life, suffering, death, and resurrection reveal how we are to live and die so that we might live abundantly. The trick is, and will always be, what that story has to do with us.

Our role in God's story simply is to keep it going. We aren't called to be clever, witty, or innovative, as much as we are called to be stewards of what we've inherited and leaders in passing it on. This would be easy if we weren't right in the middle of the story we're trying to tell. In other words, God is alive and dynamic, and the Holy Spirit blows where it will (John 3:8), which can make turning the page on which we're writing a tense, divisive, and arduous task.

When the Spirit moves it rarely makes things easy. The third person of the Trinity is hardly polite—driving Jesus into the wilderness (Mark 1:12), rushing about like a violent wind (Acts 2:2), offering holy visions of things we once thought unclean (Acts 10:15), and saying no to things we think are good ideas (Acts 16:5-7). This is why we must be stewards of hope when telling God's story. Without hope we might see the Holy Spirit's driving and rushing about as something trying to tear down instead of lift up. When Jesus breathed the Spirit upon the disciples he said, "If you forgive the sins of any, they are forgiven them; and if you retain the sins of any, they are retained" (John 20:22 NASB). What an amazing and terrifying prospect!

Our Present Reality

So what does this next page in our story look like? Let's begin with where we are. The United Methodist Church doesn't seem so united today, if it ever was. We have folks on both sides of a fence whose posts in the middle are broader than those folks looking over the fence would like to admit. In order to continue our mission of making disciples of Jesus Christ for the transformation of the world, the story we share with the world must go beyond the adjectives we use to describe where we stand. We are not called to make progressive disciples or orthodox disciples; at least when calling Simon the Zealot and Matthew the Tax Collector, Jesus didn't seem ultimately concerned with the lens through which they understood their discipleship. He simply said, "Follow me." We are the salt of the earth (Matthew 5:13), but our story loses its flavor when we equate the lens through which we interpret the gospel with the gospel itself. In other words, our story is not conservative, liberal, or centrist. Our story is the gospel, and the gospel is the source of our hope.

Regardless where The UMC finds itself in the near future, hopeful stories of Christ's transformative work is happening now and will continue to happen. Through works of justice the church is speaking truth to power. Partnering with local businesses and nonprofits is reshaping our understanding of what discipleship can be. Technology is redefining what it means to gather together as the body of Christ. Mission and outreach continue to tear down the walls we like to build between *us* and *them*. Leadership is also being found in what some might consider the least likely of places. Justice, mission, leadership, and more are the marks of hope revealing that the gospel story is a present reality. We shouldn't ignore the tension we experience when wrestling with the gospel, but our story must be saturated with hope. Otherwise, we might discover that the root of our tension is a tug-of-war over the worry, money, and power that Christ has already commanded us to lay aside.

Our hope and God's hope should be one and the same, and the only way to accomplish this is to know God's story. We begin with looking at Scripture from Genesis 1 to Revelation 22. It's important to look at the whole story in order to see God's hopeful desire for us, the world, and all that is in it. Sometimes we make the mistake of thinking that our relationship with God begins with the fall in Genesis 3, and our ending is the lake of fire in Revelation 20. Like a quilt that isn't sewn all the way to the edges, if we don't read from cover to cover, our hope in God unravels.

Hope needs help, which is why Paul surrounds hope with faith and love. Hope is a destination, faith is trusting that the destination is where God is calling you to be, and love is how you get there. Another way to see the relationship between hope, faith, and love is through story. Hope is the story we imagine, faith is the story we tell, and love is the story we live. God's Word fills us with the holy imagination to realize that all things are possible through Christ who strengthens us. Sharing this story is both our confession and the source of our pardon. Putting our hands and feet to work in building God's kingdom reveals the abundant life God desires for us all.

What tapestry is being woven in The United Methodist Church? What does the quilt we reveal to the world say about its creator? The quilt needs to be distinctly Wesleyan, but there is a sly idolatry of revealing Wesley with more clarity than God. Likewise, the quilt may look like only human hands have hold of the thread. Or, we follow one particular thread thinking that one thread is what's holding the quilt together. Our quilt should be a picture of God and neighbor with a Wesleyan pattern. In other words, it seems that half of the quilt is held in the sky and the other half is being pulled up from the earth, but God's desire is for heaven and earth to become one.

We Are Story

We must first understand that we don't make sense without story. Can you imagine sitting around the dining room table and not saying anything? Sharing stories is important to who we are because in a very real sense we are story. Have you ever considered when you say the word, *I*, what *I* is? Your identity is a collection of your experiences over time. In other words, you are a story. Your life is a story of highs and lows, victories and defeats, happiness and sorrow. Some moments in your story hold greater weight than others: birthdays, funerals, graduations, your first car accident, and the first time you fell in love. It's important to see these important life events as chapters in a larger work called *You*. Sometimes we make the mistake of taking a single chapter and thinking it defines the rest of the story. Hope can be elusive unless we think cover to cover.

Much like when we read God's story, taking a few verses out of context can leave us with a misguided picture of God. Take the story of Moses and the Golden Calf for example:

> *When Moses saw that the people were running wild (for Aaron had let them run wild, to the derision of their enemies), then Moses stood in the gate of the camp, and said, "Who is on the LORD's side? Come to me!" And all the sons of Levi gathered around him. He said to them, "Thus says the LORD, the God of Israel, 'Put your sword on your side, each of you! Go back and forth from gate to gate throughout the camp, and each of you kill your brother, your friend, and your neighbor.'" The sons of Levi did as Moses commanded, and about three thousand of the people fell on that day.*
>
> *(Exodus 32:25-28 NRSV)*

If this is our only snapshot of God, either the LORD or Moses seems to be a monster, unable to offer mercy or grace in the midst of disobedience. Three thousand people lost their life on the day Moses presented them with God's law. This story is certainly troubling, but you have to keep reading. Later in God's story, the disciples are all gathered in one place to celebrate Pentecost, the festival remembering when God offered Israel the law through Moses. On that day, the Holy Spirit was poured out upon the disciples appearing as tongues of fire resting upon each of them. The crowd heard their own language being spoken and understood without translation. Peter stands to address the crowd, and three thousand people join the church. On the day the Law was offered, three thousand people lost their life. On the day the Spirit was offered, three thousand people found their life. This doesn't necessarily make the story any easier, but when we keep reading God's story we discover that where there is death, there is life, and life has the final word. We will find hope if we keep reading.

Living through a hurricane is an exercise in hope. You watch the news with dread as meteorological models point the storm in wild and erratic directions. If the storm is headed your way, and if you're fortunate, you have a few days to either evacuate and/or board up the windows. Then the rain and the wind unrelentingly beat around the house like an angry demon showing its force. The lights go out, the fridge stops humming, the air stops circulating, and you wait. Then there is an eerie calm. You've hit the eye of the storm. Those who are new to this southern season might think the worst is over. Just as you begin to breathe a sigh of relief, the winds that were coming from the east are now coming from the west. At some point you begin to wonder whether the rising waters or the violent wind will cause the most damage. At some point, it doesn't quite matter. Then the storm does finally pass. At first you feel thankful, but it doesn't take long for a great sadness to overwhelm you. What has been damaged? What can be replaced? What will you never see again?

Stories of tragedy and hope begin long before and long after you might imagine. When we look at our lives we tend to see our story in snapshots rather than an album. Your story didn't begin when you took your first breath. Your story began when God breathed life into humanity in the beginning. Your story doesn't end when you breathe your last. Your story ends when we will see the new heaven and new earth, where pain and suffering are no more.

Some might say there's a storm brewing in The United Methodist Church. Will it be the rising waters of human sexuality or the whipping winds of biblical interpretation that causes the most damage? At a certain point, it doesn't matter. Does our story lead to thousands losing their life or finding their life? We are story, and our hope is in knowing that our story and God's story are united in the person of Jesus Christ.

How Do We Tell Our Story?

People have been telling stories as long as there have been stories to tell. Whether we pick up a paintbrush, strum a guitar, or jot down a poem, the stories we tell help us understand and interpret the world around us. Think about the second day of creation when God separated the waters above and the waters below. The dome between the waters God called Sky. (Genesis 1:6-8). Of course, we know that the sky is full of air and not water, but waters, held back above the dome of Sky, is a beautiful way to make sense of why the sky is blue and why water falls to the earth during a rainstorm. I remember getting a call from the preschool director because my daughter told her teacher, "Mommy eats babies," and the preschool director was trying to find out more information (as you might imagine). What the teacher and the director didn't know is that my wife was pregnant at the time, and this was my daughter's way of saying that there was a baby in Mommy's tummy. This made perfect (and terrifying) sense in my young daughter's worldview.

Stories help shape our understanding of the world around us, or is it the other way around? Sometimes instead of helping us understand the world, the stories we tell shape the world itself. We all hold a bias. Understanding the world necessitates interpretation. This is why word problems at the end of a math test are so important. Yes, we need to learn the mechanics of two plus two through repetition of numbers, plus signs, and equal signs, but the real world isn't so neatly arranged. Johnny has fifteen apples and Maria has three. How many apples do they have together? The obvious answer is eighteen, but in the real world we might ask some additional questions about Johnny and Maria. If you see that Johnny has fifteen and Maria has three, what's the first question you might ask about the situation? Why does Maria have fewer? Why is Johnny sharing his apples? Are the apples organic? How many are they trying to feed? Why didn't they just get bananas because bananas are cheaper?

The way we share stories matters. It is true that The United Methodist Church is declining in membership in the United States, but the way we report this membership shift shapes the way we move forward. Is the decline due to a change in theology? Could it be because of birthrate? Is the variation due to millennials having different priorities or baby boomers not willing to change or something we haven't yet discovered? Could it be that God is pruning in order to bring about rebirth?

Unfortunately, sometimes we share stories in order to place blame rather than share information. Think of the latest high-stakes political campaign. Negative ads emphasizing the sins of the other side's candidate are so prevalent because they work, but as Christians we can and must do better! The church's understanding of human sexuality certainly bears the weight of the current tension in The UMC, but the way we live into this tension can bear great fruit. If this tension is the only story we share then soon, after reports are written, petitions offered, and votes tallied, we will have nothing to share at all. *Are we a 1 issue story?*

What stories do you share about your local congregation? Are they full of hope or tragedy? Do your stories center around the budget or a building? Are these stories about the work Christ is doing through you, around you, or in spite of you? The way we share stories matters because stories shape our assumptions. If a child is told she won't succeed, chances are she won't. When United Methodist headlines exclusively share words like *schism*, *death-tsunami*, *decline*, and *trial*, our holy imagination is deprived of what the Holy Spirit might be saying.

Changing our stories isn't escapism. The goal is never to put on rose-tinted glasses while the world is falling apart, but how can we share our faith and our future in a way that invites fruitfulness instead of a barren place? For example, when we gather for Communion on Sunday mornings, I take the bread, break the bread, and say, "This is the broken body of Christ, so that you might be made whole." Without the whole sentence, we are left with little hope. At the Lord's Table we remember our past, ask for grace in the present, and seek nourishment for the future journey. We neither deny our brokenness nor ignore our commonality, yet it is the "Grand Channel" whereby we become one with Christ and one with each other. This is a story worth telling.

Our Story's Future

One of my new favorite songs is "How Do I Get There" by seventy-four-year-old Don Bryant, best known for the soulful "I Can't Stand the Rain" with Ann Peebles in 1973. Forty-four years later, Bryant penned a mournful and bluesy song asking about a place where, "we will study war no more."[1] He begins each phrase saying, "They tell me of a place…" and he ends by asking how he can get to this place. The hopeful words are undergirded by heavy, sorrowful, and repetitive music. The song reveals a poignant picture of a Job-like figure crying out to the heavens, while his feet are stuck in a cyclical and painful world going nowhere. In other words, he's lamenting that he hears stories about peace, reconciliation, and wholeness, but he certainly can't see it.

It is important to fill our stories with hope, but these stories mean little without action. We pray the Lord's Prayer daily saying, "Thy kingdom come, thy will be done on earth as it is in heaven." In other words, God's desire is for heaven and earth to be one. John of Patmos seeing a new heaven and a new earth where God and humanity live in the same place (Revelation 21:1-3) is not so much a future prophecy, but a call to action.

The church should be a "thin place" where the line between heaven and earth should be soft, porous, and permeable. Thomas Merton once said, "Life is this simple. We are living in a world that is absolutely transparent, and God is shining through it all the time.… If we abandon ourselves to God and forget ourselves, we see it sometimes, and we see it maybe frequently. God shows Himself everywhere, in everything—in people and things and in nature and in events. It becomes very obvious that God is everywhere and in everything and we cannot be without Him. It's impossible. The only thing is that we don't see it."[2]

The line between the human and Divine can be quite thin. Sometimes we think of the earth as a place for the living and heaven as a place for those who have died. Jesus blurs the line between the two, revealing that both are a place of abundant life. Jesus receives word that his beloved friend Lazarus is sick and near death, and interestingly he waits for two days before setting out on a two-day journey because, as Jesus says, "This illness isn't fatal. It's for the glory of God." After word spread that Lazarus died, Jesus travels to his home in Bethany. When he arrives, Martha, Lazarus's sister, says, "Lord, if you had been here, my brother wouldn't have died."

Isn't this a familiar phrase—"If . . ." When tragedy strikes us, when bad things happen we are quick to say "if only." "If only I had worked harder." "If only I had prayed more." "If only he had known Jesus, things would be okay." Sometimes I think we are saying this about our own United Methodist Church. If only we had been more faithful we would not be seeing decline. If only we were less institutional we could be on the move. If only we had more young clergy the church would be vibrant. If only we were more conservative or more liberal. . . . All of this might be true, but it is so very interesting that Jesus waited until Lazarus was dead so that God's glory might be seen. Through this perceived decline are we about to see God's glory revealed?

Jesus approaches the tomb, and commands that the stone be rolled away. As they prepare to roll the stone away, Mary says a curious thing—"Lord, the smell will be awful. He's been dead four days." Doing the work of God is not always sanitary. Doing the work of God is not always clean and tidy. Sometimes it's messy and difficult. Sometimes you have to get your hands dirty. Don't let your fear of stench get in the way of seeing the glory of God!

Jesus commanded Lazarus to "Come out!" As Lazarus exits the tomb, Christ commands him to be unbound. As Christians we are to live unbound lives. We do not play by the rules of the world. The world seems addicted to choosing sides, burning opponents, and living as if scarcity is our default. This cannot be our future.

The story we share matters. If the only thing we share is talk of division, left versus right, rich versus poor, or gay versus straight, we leave little room for hope. Hope is our destination, faith is trusting in that destination, and love is how we get there. If heaven is eternal, and heaven should be an earthly reality, then we must crucify language rooted in scarcity. May our stories reflect the heavenly abundance Christ is preparing for all of God's children.

What Can I Do Today?

As Christians we are called to be storytellers. Christ's story of redemption and resurrection should shine through everything we say and do. Maybe Jesus rarely mentioned hope because we are the ones to proclaim the Word? Story is how we share what we value. Every year my congregation hosts a pumpkin patch to raise funds for mission and outreach. It's true that it costs a few thousand dollars to get the softball field ready to receive the truckload of pumpkins, and when the last pumpkin is sold (or thrown away) we receive tenfold in revenue that we can share with the community, but this is not the story we tell. We lift up the families who have joined our faith community because they first ventured onto our campus to take pictures at the patch. We celebrate the children who enjoy "Story Time at the Patch" during school field trips. We call attention to the Navaho nation, which benefits from each pumpkin sold. Even though you can know a lot about the pumpkin patch from the expense and revenue spreadsheet on my computer, the story we share is something the spreadsheet is ill-equipped to communicate.

We share our hopeful stories in a lot of different ways, and you can too!

- **Worship**: Every Sunday during October, just before the offering is collected, I share a word about what happened at the patch in the previous week. Sometimes the story is about a child who ran through the pallets with reckless abandon. Sometimes I mention the interesting people we meet. Never do I share sales figures.

- **Social Media**: A picture is worth a thousand words. Sharing a smile and a pumpkin on Facebook or Twitter might be the very thing someone needs to see in their news feed.

- **Small Groups**: We are always looking for volunteers. Opening small groups with ways people can connect with one another outside of the classroom helps to spread an already infectious hope.

- **Stock Footage**: Using images from the pumpkin patch as worship backgrounds emphasizes the good news happening in the patch without having to say a word.

- **Swag**: When you buy a pumpkin, you don't leave with just a pumpkin. Everyone leaves with a thank you bag containing information about the church and how the pumpkin proceeds are being used. And, you get a fancy Asbury magnet to share with a friend

- **Synergy**: We don't just sell pumpkins at the pumpkin patch. We also sell salsa made by the Methodist Children's Home, which is an easy way to share stories of how the Children's Home is changing the world.

It seems that talk about politics, discipline, division, and tension disappear from our stories when you are working the pumpkin patch. It's difficult to hold the baggage we like to carry around when your hands are full moving pumpkins around. Worship, social media, and small groups are great ways to share the hope you see happening around you, and this is where The UMC is at its best!

Communion Is Our Story

Every chapter throughout this book will end with a word about Communion and a litany that you might use in worship. Holy Communion is the "Grand Channel" through which we receive the real presence and the grace of Jesus Christ. Especially when we find ourselves in the midst of division, antagonism, and brokenness, the Lord's Table calls us back to "re-member" the body of Christ through forgiveness, reconciliation, and peace. Some say that The UMC must be broken apart in order to move forward, but our hope is that the bread is the only thing that needs to be broken in our story. In large part, Holy Communion is our story. We gather to confess our sins and receive the good news of forgiveness. We proclaim what God through Christ in the power of the Holy Spirit has done, is doing, and will do. We respond by approaching the Table to receive the broken bread and the wine outpoured. Finally, we are sent forth to proclaim the story we have received so the world might know the hope God desires for all.

Communion Litany

As we gather around the Table we remember God
Creator of everything seen and unseen,
Author of our story as heirs in Christ

Who offers us hope as a destination,
Faith to trust in your direction,
And Love as the way to get where we need to be.

And so, with your people on earth, and all the company of heaven
We praise your name, and join in their unending hymn:

Holy, holy, holy, Lord, God of power and might,
Heaven and earth are full of your glory.
Hosanna in the highest!
Blessed is the one who comes in the name of the Lord
Hosanna in the highest!

Holy are you and blessed is your Son, Jesus Christ,
Who put on flesh and walked among us,
To reveal your story of justice, mercy, and salvation.
He took bread from the earth,
And gave it new meaning by breaking it
And naming it his body
Making it the bread from heaven broken for us
After supper he took the cup,
And gave it a new story by naming it his blood poured out for us
When we break the bread and share the wine we remember Christ,
Re-member the body of Christ,
And remember God's story and our place within it
To proclaim the mystery of faith.

Christ has died, Christ is risen, Christ will come again.

Pour out your Holy Spirit upon us gathered here,
And on these gifts of bread and wine
That we might be nourished
To together tell your story of hope, through faith, in love.

Through your Son, Jesus Christ,
With the Holy Spirit, in your holy Church
All honor and glory is yours, Almighty God,
Now and forever. Amen.

Chapter Two

PARTNERSHIPS WITH PURPOSE

Katie McKay Simpson

Social entrepreneurs might just prove to be the missing
missionaries that we need for a fair and just society.
—Dr. R.K. Pachauri, Skoll World Forum 2009 address

My family is filled with community leaders and entre-preneurs—I grew up watching each of my five older brothers and sisters start their own businesses or firms and thrive in the ventures to which they committed their lives. Some ventures suceeded, others died. All the while, they continued to improve in both their skill and resolve, learn from their failures, and hone their craft. And many have used their business not just for profit, but for good in our community. My brother Matt, who owns car dealerships, created an automotive vocational technical school in the most depressed part of my childhood hometown to offer viable opportunities for young men and women who aren't college-bound to gain a skill to earn a living wage for their families.

As I was sitting there at the dedication for the school, I thought about how this infusion of capital would change the course of young people's lives in an economically depressed community. I found myself asking, "Why is the church not doing this kind of work? It's a shame that I am not nearly as inspired by the conversations we are having in my church or in my denomination as I am about the vision that is being made real in this moment."

This has always been a tension for me. In college (and if I'm completely honest, on the hard days in ministry too) I struggled with whether my life would be better served in the business sector or in law or journalism rather than ministry, as if those "secular" jobs and my potential life as a pastor would be somehow work at cross-purposes.

The question at the root of the struggle was, "what kind of work in the world will offer me the greatest capacity, potential, and opportunity to affect the most change to better the world for the most people?" As I've chosen to answer the call to serve God through The United Methodist Church with my life, this question is still very much alive within.

During General Conference 2012 in the bleachers as a reserve clergy delegate, I was waiting for my turn to sit in to vote on behalf of colleagues. At the time, I was gleefully expecting my first child—twenty-four weeks along—and I could feel her kicking while I heard the thorough reports and testimonies of denominational leaders giving a dismal picture of the future. We were trying, you may recall, to restructure our denominational system in anticipation of the coming "death tsunami" that suggested our United Methodist Church would be nonexistent by 2054 if the present trajectory of membership decline continues. I was a newly ordained pastor then, with my whole life of ministry as an elder leading local churches still ahead, and all evidence would suggest that these reports should not be seen as good news.

And yet, I firmly believed this is the best thing that could ever happen to us.

I know. It seems crazy—possibly flippant in fact, to some.

However, I knew then as I've come to discover again and again through the ups and downs of ministry and life that we do not always have to fear what people tell us to fear. I've come to know and see that with every death, there is a hope-filled rebirth—a new possibility ready to emerge right under the surface.

It is a strange and disturbing thing when an ordained elder like myself, who deeply loves The United Methodist Church, is more inspired by the "secular" social ventures that give hope, opportunity, and a new start on life to the young men and women in my hometown than the conversations my denomination is having on the world's stage at General Conference.

I've asked myself, *Is there something wrong with me? Wrong with that?*

Or might there be something right—even the call of God and the rushing inspiration of the Holy Spirit within this new awareness?

What Is Social Entrepreneurship?

We as faith communities find ourselves facing an unfamiliar wilderness. In the midst of this wilderness, our denomination's leaders call boldly for "entrepreneurial leadership." My guess is half of the denomination is still wondering what that means, and why it really matters. I believe that social entrepreneurship is a major, in fact, undeniable key to our revitalization as a church.

Social entrepreneurship is an emerging trend within both the business and nonprofit worlds of pursuing practical solutions to social problems. United Methodist Bishop John Schol reflected, "For Christian leaders, this blending of business ideas with Christian mission can be a valuable tool to help sustain communities and an organization while at the same time bearing witness to the reign of God."[1] There are a variety of examples of what falls under the umbrella of social entrepreneurship—everything from microlender Kiva to shoe-retailer TOMS to solar lamp manufacturer KARIBU, according to one post on the UM & Global website.[2] The church is beginning to discover that businesses don't get to "corner the market" on being branded as agents of change, but we can instead reclaim that trademark for ourselves.

This is where we come to the opportunity for social entrepreneurship. If you ask me what a theological definition of social entrepreneurship might be, I would immediately go to the passage in Acts 1:22, "must become along with us a witness to his resurrection." In the wake of death, they were searching for new leaders that would have the right posture and narrative to make lasting change in the communities they enter anew and live within—breaking down barriers, preaching that God always makes a way when there seems to be no way, and connecting those who usually would not find themselves at Table together as family around a common purpose.

God intends for the enterprise of Christians to extend outward, taking the Great Commission seriously and literally. More and more, the churches making a lasting difference are the ones realizing the answers for this next chapter of our church's thriving lie beyond the knowledge inside our walls and doors. The mission lies outside of the borders between the church and our communities that we, in fact, over decades and centuries of church growth, have created. We must now gain the courage to begin flirting with the edges of what we know.

The Present Reality

Cultural changes such as globalization, the rise of technology, and urban sprawl have all contributed to our own collective marginalization as a church from being the center of authority, activity, and influence our communities once enjoyed. We find ourselves where we are in our wounded and anxious church today, limping along as if much hope is lost. I continue to be surrounded by the narrative from others, "If only families would value faith once again, and people would come back, we would not have to deal with these issues we are facing today." This narrative is spun as if it is the job of the community around us to bring new life into the church, rather than new life being offered the other way around.

There is often no shortage of creativity or ideas in churches about how we might reach out to the community and offer hope and change in new ways. However, when the roof is leaking and financial giving is down, and the committed base of those who serve continues to age in most United Methodist congregations, we find underfunded visions, staff cuts, and congregational burnout tend to rule in the lives of our small to midsize communities of faith. How can churches reinvent their approach to the social problems in our mission field when their own internal problems seem just too much to bear?

These realities in our churches and in the culture around us are real. And yet, I believe firmly that the local church is still the greatest hope of the world. It is made up of believers committed to living out the gospel message of Jesus Christ. The church has the greatest potential to effect change and better the lives of individuals and families in our communities.

So let's put on a hopeful lens for a moment to this reality in which we now stand: if the death of the church is, in fact, imminent, this death would provide an unexpected opportunity once again for new life—to return to our roots. The Wesleyan movement at its best has always been an ecosystem where we've developed partnerships with people throughout life's circumstances and across disciplines—relationships from birth to death that rely on each other to thrive. We are being called once again to be witnesses to the power of resurrection, but to establish the work in a new form for a new age.

There is hope. Here are the places of hope I find as this growing awareness is emerging.

The Key To Our Salvation Is in Our Heritage And Mission.

What is our mission statement?

"To make disciples of Jesus Christ for the transformation of the world," right?

As a church, we focus a great deal on discipleship, but transformation? Real transformation that is beyond a mission trip and speaking out on a picket line for a social cause? This transformation that we seek requires a commitment of relationships, finances, and time that is much deeper, more enduring.

The language of social entrepreneurship may be new, but the concept is not. We have always had social entrepreneurs, even if we did not call them by that name. The United Methodist Church (or, in this case, its predecessor forms) has had a strain of this throughout its life. Dr. Thomas B. Welch and the creation of Welch's Grape Juice is an early example of entrepreneurship to effect social change. "In the 1800s, churches faced a dilemma. To combat the epidemic of alcoholism, the temperance movement advocated total abstinence from all alcohol. In celebration of the Lord's Supper though, the church filled the Communion chalice with wine." Welch's unfermented grape juice was created to battle the effects of alcohol on families, particularly with the economic impact that addiction was causing for families during the temperance movement, which the General Conference played a key role in by creating a Board of Temperance, Prohibition, and Public Morals. Methodist women like Frances Willard also worked in partnership with Welch to ensure this option was available and made mainstream. "In 1864, the General Conference of The Methodist Episcopal Church entered the conversation when they approved a report from the Temperance Committee that recommended 'the pure juice of the grape be used in the celebration of the Lord's Supper.'" In the 1880s, *The Book of Discipline* was finally changed to reflect this movement started by a dentist that turned into a business that impacted thousands of communities in North America to date.[3]

With this potential to be change agents at hand, every week with my staff, I ask the question, "Where, in our ministry this week, did we see a transformed life? Or developing evidence of a transformed community?" Some weeks, there are a plethora of stories. Others, there is nothing to be shared. On the weeks where those testimonies are hard to find, I ask the staff to do an assessment of time to truly direct their work toward the formation and transformation of people. Gone are the days where the church can remain siloed and separated from the rest of our community and expect to thrive.

The truth is, the answer is both within us and outside of us.

Within us, meaning we have to be clear about the human resources we have at our disposal within the church to leverage for the community's best good. Then considering the needs outside of us, we must find a fertile ground in relationships, financial viability, need, facilities, and timing.

To give an example, my congregation has started an effort that is a community partnership with the strong possibility of becoming an entrepreneurial venture at Barbe Elementary in Lake Charles as we partner with them to combat low literacy rates. We discovered that our congregation had a human resource of thirty-two retired teachers, most still passionate about teaching, which we could deploy to fight the battle for literacy. Then, through community connections, we became aware of a failing school with an administration that was open, enthusiastic, and permission-giving. We started with young girls beginning a summer program in literacy and character development (this was a unique gap we had the opportunity to fill—there were already many education enrichment classes for boys to keep them in school and off the streets). This program as it develops has a strong possibility of becoming intergenerational and a revenue-producing venture that might provide opportunities to reinvest in new education efforts in our city.

Considering the call to transformation of our mission statement, social entrepreneurship is key to getting churches out of the Band-Aid rut of giving school supplies and checks with no relationship attached, or creating cultures of benevolence that keep the poor coming back for more rather than the church coming alongside and equipping them to lead their lives, with the church in support and encouragement every step of the way.

There are many different examples of United Methodists beginning to understand the value social entrepreneurship brings:

There are potable water wells dug in Africa by Ginghamsburg Church and other churches who have made these long-lasting international relationships. Glide in San Francisco has a team on staff of fifteen social entrepreneur interns under the age of thirty-five with backgrounds including media, web development, marketing, finance, sports, and education to effect social change. Union Coffee in Dallas creates a space for revenue to be created for causes like eradicating hunger, encouraging literacy, reducing the rate of partner violence, and curbing youth incarceration. Also in Dallas, Safe Spaces Lebanon was started by a group of United Methodists who were struck by the trauma experienced by women and children who are Syrian refugees in Lebanon. They now, through a cooperative effort, have created a nonprofit that is rebuilding a school which will provide educational and psychosocial support for these families. Caritas House in Memphis was connected to Everette Memorial UMC, working to build trust and provide a positive alternative for the neighborhood children of different ethnic and socioeconomic backgrounds through engagement with music, hospitality, and theatre. No doubt, there are many more. God is calling us to remember our heritage and live into the mission that we already claim for our life together to continue the revival that has already begun.

Openness to New Forms.

It is said that every problem has the potential to turn into an opportunity. Well, the state of the Church is most certainly one of the greatest perceived deaths that ultimately has the potential to bring new life to us all. The gospel reminds us that to live, we must die to an old form and experience the surprising life that is in store as we open to a new way of seeing, relating, and connecting to our mission field. Congregations are beginning, albeit slowly, to wake up to the opportunities around them. There is already everything we could need in our communities to revive our ministries and thrive if only we have the courage to get out of our church walls and look for it.

I was hosting a conversation at one of our major universities with thirty college students and young adults seeking to know more about avenues for ministry. I was prepared to talk about traditional avenues of ordination, licensing, and so on; however, more than half were asking primarily about roles outside of the church—ways they can be bi-vocational working for a church and then own a restaurant or work as a social worker or missionary. The same trend is happening among millennial generations primarily in our theological schools—young people abandoning the ordination process because they have this hunch that there is a better, more innovative means of changing the world. They generally see the church as unfit or unwilling to empower them in these ventures—and to this point, our present reality would suggest that is true.

But it doesn't have to be that way.

I was trained for a good while in church planting, which also helps the church to get outside of the walls, but instead of an investment in creating the foundation for a new church community and facilities, along with other resources, social innovation is "an investment in people, chiefly by resourcing clergy and lay leaders through coaching, training, supervision and equipping," as Bishop Kenneth Carder said.[4] One way annual conferences and local churches are being equipped is to offer grants, such as "Fresh Expressions" grants that are available across much of the connection.

We can see other faith communities begin to "wake up" to this reality while we are still trying to hold on to old forms. After a trip to London three years back, I found a couple of examples that deeply confirmed this for me. First, I found myself standing with a number of other ministry colleagues from The United Methodist Church to meet with Shannon Hopkins, from Matryoshka Haus, an organization whose purpose is to create training opportunities for faithful people to interact with their surrounding cities and towns to help heal and transform social problems. I found myself sitting in St. Mary Aldermary Church drinking cappuccino in pews that were turned to face each other for conversation rather than forward to hear one professional religious person tell the gospel story as in days past. It represented a marked change in the way churches are invited to relate to the world around us. An old cathedral refreshed to reach a new age—in the middle of a bustling metropolis creating a revenue-producing venture that honors the voices of many to bless and transform the world around them. Not just creating another program. Re-creating the church, its mission, and vision focus from the outside in.

Gil Rendle noted that in 2008, among the thirty-five thousand local churches of United Methodism in the United States, ten thousand had thirty-five or fewer in average worship attendance.[5] Clergy and lay leaders will have to shift the focus toward the mission that is both within the walls of the church and the mission that is outside it. Laity will have to be disciples and deployed in new ways to live the gospel and effect social change through leveraging their sphere of influence created through community organizations and their workplaces.

Because we know that the learnings from social innovation will be crucial for the church to continue its witness to the communities surrounding us in relevant ways, it would be a wise and hope-filled move to begin as a connection to allow for more bi-vocational credentialed clergy or offer more financial support for those that do the work of social entrepreneurship in the church full-time. There are many contexts that will not require an appointed pastor's full-time energy—this would be a great way to use their giftedness and passion for ministry effectively.

We will ultimately need a different input to expect an updated output. What could we gain if bishops and district superintendents were free to spend less time on administrative matters and more time mobilizing congregations to partner with change agents in our districts, annual conferences, and various countries?

What if our seminaries trained pastors in the art of community organizing, nonprofit management, and sustainable investment practices? Or, partnered beyond fumbling through the maze of a dual degree to offer the wisdom and benefit of training from a business school or social work program as an integrated aspect of our own formation? The kind of pastor that would emerge would be vastly different than the "product" that is created today.

Fund-raising for Community Transformation Shifting

Social ventures generally seek to change the world while also generating a profit and being financially sustainable.

The way we think about fund-raising for community transformation through our church's ministry must change. I have been the pastor of a midsize Methodist congregation for three years. In that time, I am starting to see the barriers and battles regular pastors and engaged lay leaders encounter everyday. We want to staff for growth, but there seems to be not enough money, the congregation is burned out and overtaxed, and other excuses come, such as, "we can't pay insurance on a second pastor to expand our ministry," and so on. What would happen if churches and denominations invested in social venture start-ups rather than more staff members to prop up our over-programmed congregations?

It is true that millennials aren't giving to support ministry as generously as previous generations—are they even coming to church on a regular basis? We see fewer and fewer visitors. This is where a grassroots effort and vital witness of the local church can save us—no program or decree from judicatories or effort from general agencies will save us. The good news, and hard news, is that every day men and women in local congregations have great agency in this critical conjuncture of our church's future—and the choices we make, well, will make all the difference.

I had the opportunity to speak with Sam Wells, former dean of the Chapel at Duke University and now rector at St. Martin-in-the-Fields on a trip with other United Methodist pastors about three years ago. In one of our discussions about ministry in the postmodern world, he reminded me that the church has always—whether proactively or reactively—shifted its way of providing for ministry to reach a new age. Early in Christian congregations, priests operated on a patronage system. This system relied on the generosity of one well-off family to support, and in some ways, direct the ministry of the church. Then churches moved from a patronage system to a stewardship system that we are more familiar with today in most congregations.

However, today we are shifting into a new reality of creating revenue-producing systems to support ministry and stay relevant in today's world. This is the kind of effort most churches cannot accomplish on their own. It will require us to venture outside of our doors and connect with those around us—as those at

St. Martin-in-the-Fields have done by offering encounters where spirituality intersects with music and the arts. Every day one finds hundreds of families and business people on their lunch breaks eating from a cafeteria in the ancient Crypt. Again, old systems repurposing their space and resources to encounter their communities in ways that years ago none of us could have ever dreamed.

One example of how this is already happening in The United Methodist Church is in Côte d'Ivoire, West Africa. The United Methodist News Service published an article in 2014 on how members of United Methodist Women (UMW) there are partnering with the social entrepreneur mobile phone company Pubcell CI to earn money for UMW's initiatives around the world. Members sign up for the mobile phone service, which then shares revenue from ads that are displayed on users' phones.

UMW is using the money earned from Pubcell plus an additional $1,000 grant from Pubcell to support women who want to start business endeavors—almost like a microloan program as we've witnessed gaining success in other parts of the world. This partnership provides a source of income so that they can lift themselves out of poverty. According to the website post, not long ago, outreach in Africa looked like "Western experts coming in to plan and execute large-scale infrastructure projects. This... represents the future of mission-led development in Africa: African women banding together to conduct their own small-scale social entrepreneurship projects."[6]

The church that faces seeming "death" in one area of the world is experiencing new life in unexpected ways through these purposeful partnerships. A friend and fellow social entrepreneur, Mike Baughman, as the "community curator" of Union Coffeehouse, Dallas, said this:

Social entrepreneurs are a thriving community of world changers who are interested in converting profits and industry into love. The church shares with them a common mission: the transformation of the world. And though we may not be as effective at transforming the world as we once were, we have the very things that most social ventures need: property, people, funding and a narrative of servanthood.[7]

We have to gain the courage to channel our church resources in new ways when opportunities for response arise. That can prove difficult at times, but it can be the very source, or seed, of growth and trust that has the potential to affect the the common good of all.

The Unintended Consequence of Social Entrepreneurship

As we seek to transform and change the world around us, I find that churches also are changed from within because they courageously chose to engage in this work. I have been a pastor in three congregations—and each of these churches has been "stuck" to one degree or another. The causes included crippling debt, mistrust stemming from sexual misconduct from a previous pastor, deferred maintenance on buildings, and congregational decline. In their "stuck" stage, there was crippling conflict, a drop in giving and attendance, and a lack of vision.

The good news is that social enterprise—creating purposeful partnerships—can free us to be the church God has always intended us to be. By looking outward, we might be surprised that the conflict that has held us back from our mission in the past begins on the road to healing. I have a friend and mentor in ministry, the Reverend Dr. Craig Gilliam, who has helped me see that churches are being held back by anxiety. He says, "Anxiety limits our options, strangles creativity, restricts our vision of what is possible, and removes us from the moment where what needs to happen is emerging. When anxiety is high, we view change as a threat and the unfamiliar as a mortal enemy. Ultimately, when anxiety catches us, like the static on the radio, our perceptions become distorted."[8]

Social entrepreneurship builds trust in our communities and in our congregations. It also builds an entrepreneurial spirit that all of our churches must seek to regain. Creating purposeful partnerships allows us to commune deeply with those in our mission field. This work nicks away at the concept of "us and them" in our cities, and we might even find that in turning outward some of our own agenda battles that are indicative of anxious, inward-focused congregations are healed as well.

Moving toward a mind-set of abundance can lead us in even the most under-resourced context to discover there are more assets at our disposal than we could originally see. At the church I serve presently, there is an empty field on the side of our campus. Some of my faith-filled congregation have suggested we sell it. But that barren space in the middle of a growing city center begs the question: What could God do with it? What new venture will be birthed from this unused canvas with so much potential and opportunity, and how might we as the people of God be called out in powerful ways through participating in God's vision for it?

The church has had predictable conversations about how we might use this land, and they would say, "build a parking lot, a fellowship hall, or another building for more classrooms..." But lately, there have been some emerging conversations about where our passion as a church will begin to meet the world's greatest need. Lately, we have begun conversations about creating low-income housing projects for the rising rental prices in town, or a facility to house a prisoner's transition program for those trying to reenter life in their communities and the workforce that can often be unrelenting and offer little to no support for those that have had a record. With many retired teachers in our congregation, we have talked about how we can use that land to create further opportunities to expand our already thriving intergenerational continuing education programs for low-income young women and their families.

These conversations have all come by looking beyond our own needs to find how our gospel call has the opening in this time and place to address the desperate needs of others. We are all called to look beyond our own interests to assess the canvas of human and financial assets available to us to be catalysts for transformation and change. In fact, the canvas of our very lives is that which God has called us to pay deep attention to and steward well—for God's transformation to be enacted, and for human beings in each of our contexts to thrive.

How can we create these kinds of realities if we don't already notice them in front of us? Start with where you have influence. If you are a layperson, support your pastor as a dreamer and help to hold the questions of possibility so your pastor may feel companioned in moving your church forward in new ways. If you are a pastor, start developing leaders alongside you to aid in changing the structure of power from the very core of the church— starting with your staff and administrative teams to encourage innovation and collaboration in all you do.

The greatest resource the church has for accomplishing purposeful partnerships that make a positive impact and change in this world is you.

God has called you.

How can you—today—be a good steward of ourselves, the relationships and influence we have for the thriving of those in the community around us?

Difficulty in the Present Division

As we struggle to find unity in a wounded, fractured church, it is imperative that we as Methodists remain rooted in who we are—those that are committed both to, as John Wesley would say, vital piety and to social holiness.

Congregations pursuing this work to usher in the reign of God must hold as a continued priority a personal commitment to holy living and, corporately, the discipleship formation of its people that gives us the fuel, passion, fruit of the Spirit, and focus for the work of transformation outside our walls. I've heard it said, "Only transformed people transform people." Without this, social entrepreneurship ventures will lose their vitality and connection to the congregations' witness.

When Wesley says that holiness is "social" he means that the depth of our love for God is revealed by the way we love whom God loves. The writer of 1 John 4 describes the social nature of holiness: "We love because he first loved us. Those who say, 'I love God,' and hate their brothers or sisters, are liars; for those who do not love a brother or sister whom they have seen, cannot love God whom they have not seen. The commandment we have from him is this: those who love God must love their brothers and sisters also" (verses 19-21 NRSV). In the midst of denominational division, churches must do some deeper work of discernment on those places and people to which we as congregations are called, and those, too, that we fear. It may be that the neighbor whom God is calling us to serve is exactly the one that we trust and understand the least.

Social entrepreneurship focuses the vision of churches because we focus our time and resources on that which will make the greatest impact for the reign of God coming, but this work of creating, maintaining, and following vision is seldom easy. Congregations and nonprofits committed to this work must always be wary of losing focus on why we are doing this work in the first place. Ask questions like: What, in this work, makes us unique to another community organization in offering a witness to the power of the Resurrection? Toward what end are we moving? Who and what is energizing our work? Focusing and aligning our work toward a new vision requires a church to collectively commit to saying a purposeful no to good opportunities with a congregation's time and finances, to begin saying the holy yes to the new venture that God is calling you to become a part of in the effort of solving. All of this work can be accomplished regardless of denominational conversations, divisions, and decisions made—where vital local congregations continue to model and lead what "being the church" truly is all about from the ground, up.

What You Can Do Today

Be mindful about cultivating your church's resources—not just financial, but human. What are people's gifts? How can you match that individual and collective gifting with the community around you? Come to understand the occupations, skill sets, and spiritual gifts your core leaders have, and then have them extend that invitation to the congregation.

Discipline of being in "the world": Have your lay teams (and your pastor) cultivate a discipline of doing your work out in the field to reach new people. This is one of the best ways to find out what is truly happening and what the needs are in your community to make the livelihood of all around you better. Consultant

Steve James, in his training on reaching new people, often says that even taking a finance committee out to dinner during the meeting can begin to change the way one might deploy a church's funds from an inward focus to an outward focus.

Learn the value of the one to one. I was a community organizer in a labor union before I became a pastor. I found that people's stories and perspectives are key to challenging my own operating assumptions about a city, a boss, a workplace, or a social problem. There is no better tool that you have in your belt than listening—whether lay or clergy—to find out where your church's passion meets your neighborhood or city's greatest need (and it may not always be in the place you might expect or in the place that is most comfortable for your people). Still, God's call is to develop a holy boldness in your congregation for people to take that initiative to increase the ecosystem of relationships on which your church relies.

Start small: Getting to yes on beginning efforts of social entrepreneurship doesn't require consensus (yet). If you sense a resistance in your church to go about this work, start with a team, a department, or a staff person accountable to pursuing pattern-breaking change in your community, while the rest of the church focuses on other standard activities in your church's work of discipleship. The rest of the body will learn from your initial gains and enthusiasm, which will lower anxiety and, hopefully, by the power of the Spirit increase openness to what may be possible.

Develop the courageous discipline of asking for help. Social entrepreneurs can't transform inmate recidivism rates, pollution, hunger, unemployment, addiction, and homelessness by themselves. Purposeful partnerships that last will leverage the gifts and connections of all in our community—decentralizing the locus of vision, decision, engagement, and power from one to many.

Communion

Engaging in efforts of social entrepreneurship is communion itself. It is communion with our neighbors, communion with those that are different from us, and renewed communion with a more energized, Spirit-led version of each of our congregations.

It is communion as we respond to the shifts in culture and people around us by listening with compassion and curiosity.

It is communion when we grow to believe that our thriving is inextricably linked to the thriving of the community around us—economically, physically, socially, artistically, and spiritually. One cannot fully exist without the other.

It is communion when we find ourselves not as victims of the change we find around us, but instead the victors of the change that comes in our world today.

It is communion with others who, like yourself, have a desire to blaze a trail for the common good and have not let the idea die in a graveyard.

It is communion that we find when we change a life.

It is also communion with God and God's ultimate purpose.

John Wesley talked about Communion as a converting sacrament. That the Table is open wide for anyone to come so that they might encounter Jesus for the first time. No litmus test, no preparatory class, just a willing soul ready to connect with a new experience of the holy as they are called to stand up and move toward the place God bids. That act of being converted from a narrative of death and despair to one of hope and possibility is that which will save us. It is that first step forward away from the malaise of the past and toward the opportunities of the future that takes unimaginable courage in itself. And it is that level of courage that it will take for our churches to reform ourselves for a new age of making disciples of Jesus Christ for the transformation of the world.

Communion Prayer

God of change and innovation, in the turning of creation, the shifting of the seasons, from the witness of Scripture, we are keenly aware that You love us where we are, but refuse to allow us to stay there. May we believe again that Your power to turn chaos into order, to bring life from seeming death, is ours as well when we, the Body of Christ, serve as Your guided hands and feet in the world. May our desire to serve You in refreshed ways be met with Your vision for the next steps. May our concern for our own security and fixation on our scarcity be met with the abundant awareness of the needs of others. May we offer ourselves in praise and thanksgiving as a holy and living sacrifice, in union with Christ's offering for us as we witness to the mystery of faith, and serve as a bridge that connects culture to culture, problem to solution, those with much with those with little, that Your name may be glorified in all we do. In the name of Jesus, who showed us the way, Amen.

Chapter Three
THE LANGUAGE OF JUSTICE

Juan Huertas

To struggle for Justice is to pray.
—Ada Maria Isasi-Diaz

Language shapes us in ways that at times are hard to understand. The formative years of my life were spent immersed in Spanish, the language of my birth. I still have my first Bible given to me by my parents for my kindergarten graduation. In it they inscribed "May the teachings of this book make all your desires possible." Since that moment I have been engrossed in the stories told there and in the words used. The stories found there have shaped my life in ways difficult to express.

In middle school I was introduced to the Bible in English. The King James Version was required reading in the English-speaking school that I attended. I memorized chapters and tried to learn this new language through it. I quickly found that the stories of

Scripture in English did not have the warmth and depth that my Spanish Bible displayed.

It would take years for me to realize that translations matter. That individually or as a group, translators make choices, interpret, and give meaning. The task is a difficult one and it does shape the way that we as hearers and readers experience the text. The fact that we are dealing with a sacred text makes this an even more important element for all of us to consider as we struggle together with what the Bible means for us today.

Our Present Reality

In most of our communities we can easily spot the churches, but we can also easily see the places where the church is needed. There are the neighborhoods that we are afraid to drive through, the reports of the painful social situations, and the front pages of local papers. Our hearts break as we face our powerlessness but are then troubled when we open the pages of our sacred story calling us to be agents of God's presence, agents of hope.

In Spanish hope is *esperanza*, literally a state of waiting. So imagine how we would read the title of this book, we would say "The Mark of Our State of Waiting." The title itself becomes generative, feeding the imagination. What are we waiting for? What does this state look like? What characterizes this waiting state?

Hope (a state of waiting) requires a posture in each of us as individuals and especially in our life together as congregations: as we worship together, live life together, and are reminded of our identity. It's an identity shaped by the Holy Spirit into what it means to be a Christian community in the world. As we are shaped, our hope grows and as it grows we begin to behave as a *hope-full* people in the world.

It is easy to see some of the other aspects in this book as a mark of hope, but what about justice?

No moral perfection, no purity, instead, doing what God does. God healing, restoring, reminding, and making the rough places smooth and the high places flat; God bringing freedom to those who find themselves in slavery, oppressed and forgotten. This call should permeate all of what we do in the life of congregations; it should be at the center of our discipleship processes, especially among children and youth. It is this prioritizing that creates the space for justice to become a mark of hope

For forty years our denomination has been in disagreement about our response to LGBTQ people in our life as a church. There have been commissions, studies, legislation, articles, disappointments, and tears. Division has been growing within our faith communities at the same rate that is growing in our culture. Instead of being one body, one people, who follow one Lord, we have become fractured—our primary identity not rooted in discipleship but in a particular label. Most often that labeling separates justice from our understanding of discipleship.

Justice and Discipleship Do Mix

The separation of justice from discipleship has often led us into giving over justice work to nonreligious institutions in our communities and to think of justice only in juridical terms. We imagine it like a *Law & Order* episode with judges, lawyers, good people, and bad people. Often we hear justice and what we hear is revenge, payback, and people getting what they deserve.

I grew up reading justice all over the biblical story. The idea of *justicia* was part and parcel of all of the biblical witness. The English translators decided to render δικαιοσύνη (*dikaiosyne*—justice)

as *righteousness*, which in today's English has the connotation of moral perfection, purity, and/or holiness. In other words for me justice was the fruit of the work of the Holy Spirit in the lives of disciples, a primary pathway for creation to experience salvation. Justice is about doing what God requires:

> *He has told you, human one, what is good and*
> *what the LORD requires from you:*
> *to do justice, embrace faithful love, and*
> *walk humbly with your God.*
>
> *(Micah 6:8)*

Out of this misunderstanding we then tend to identify ourselves as "Social Justice" people and in United Methodism as either people rooted in social justice or in holiness as if these terms were mutually exclusive. Yet the work of holiness, or growing more deeply in the love of God, self, and neighbor, the work of becoming more distinctly set apart for the work of God's kingdom, is a work of just practice, of doing what is right for the life of the world.

Helping the needy, advocating for the voiceless, and providing food for the hungry is the work of salvation. Making sure that people have health care, that the stranger is welcomed, and the forgotten remembered is the work of salvation. Calling the religious and their leaders to faithfulness, to pay attention to their religious text, and to their own renewal is the work of salvation.

Justice is Relationship

In his book *Doing Christian Ethics from the Margins*, Dr. Miguel A. de la Torre, tells us that justice is "how a real relationship between two parties (God and human, human and human, nature and human, and /or human and society) is conducted."[1]

Justice is about relationships, so it is about the gospel, and it is about our work as bearers of the gospel. As de la Torre later tells us, "Right relationship with God is possible only if people act justly toward one another." So we as God's people, as people growing in love of God and neighbor, as people called to an ever-growing sanctified life, must be growing as a people of justice. An important question that we might ask at this point is: Are we in "right relationship" as the baptized community? In our congregations? In our denominations? Across the Christian tradition?

Our founder John Wesley called his followers not to an individual religion but to a social one, one that required community for our growth in love. Wesley knew that only together could we sustain our relationship with God. Only together in hearing of each other's stories, and hearing of God's work in others, could we humbly accept our own.

Living life together breaks us from our tendency to pride, self-centeredness, and isolation. Our tendency is to live only in worlds that are just like us, in worlds that construct a God that sees what we see, feels what we feel, and behaves like we behave. Justice and right relationship are born in our encounters and shared life with one another. Shared life that mimics God's kingdom, God's promise of wholeness (shalom) that mimics the beauty in difference.

This is why in our baptismal services we renounce the divisive, exploitative, and self-serving tendencies of our human condition and instead claim the freedom to live in a new way, a just way in the world. A way that, by the power of the Holy Spirit, makes us more true to who God created us to be and more whole—complete, healed in our relationships with God, ourselves, and neighbor.

> On behalf of the whole church, I ask you: Do you renounce the spiritual forces of wickedness, reject the evil powers of this world, and repent of your sin? . . .

> Do you accept the freedom and power God gives you to resist evil, injustice, and oppression in whatever forms they present themselves? . . .

> Do you confess Jesus Christ as your Savior, put your whole trust in his grace, and promise to serve him as your Lord, in union with the church which Christ has opened to people of all ages, nations, and races? . . . [2]

We as people of God, like the people of Israel before us, have been commissioned and empowered to renounce, repent, and resist. We do so as a sign and symbol of our new life in Christ. This empowerment serves to make us agents, coworkers with God in the restoration of all things—making right, modeling what that right being looks like, paying attention around us to come alongside others to make justice, reconciliation, healing, and goodness known and visible.

Sin is enmity, wrong relationship, broken relationships, and disordered relationships. So it makes sense that salvation is found when justice is practiced, when right relationships in our world are demanded, and when we grow as just people. Justice is gospel, justice is salvation, justice is a mark of hope. This is not anything new; in fact, hope grows when we remind each other that we are community and that being community means right relationship, being community requires justice.

Justice Is God's Image Stamped on Us

God's nature is relational and since we are made in God's image, we are relational people. From the beginning, our story has been about relationship. We are made to be with God, we are made to be with one another, and we are made to be with creation. The fall narrative in Genesis 3 is a story of broken relationships, of sowing the seeds of separation, the seeds of injustice, "Did God really say that you shouldn't eat from any tree in the garden?" (verse 1). Is God to be trusted? You need to look out for yourself first because God has an agenda! You can make the decision for yourself, if it looks good to you, that's all that matters! God is holding out, God only wants to prevent you from being like God.

Our primal story gives us the blueprint for our inclination to sin and death, but it also gives us the blueprint for our salvation. From that beginning we see again and again that God cares for *all* and for how all of us can be restored into relationships. We need to become familiar with these markers of justice in God's story:

- Immediately after the fall, humanity is given the basics they need to face the world—God reaches out to restore relationships.
- Jealousy causes Cain to kill Abel and yet God keeps Cain from being killed.
- God wanted to destroy the earth, yet God had approved of Noah and his family. God provided a way forward for them; God again restoring relationships.
- Abraham is chosen as the father of the people of Israel. As such he is given the instructions about what it means to live into his identity in God's cosmic story. We are told: "I have formed a relationship with him so that he will instruct his children and his household after him. And they will keep to the LORD's path, being moral and just so that the LORD can do for Abraham everything he said he would" (Genesis 18:19).

The Lord's path is being moral (not pure but living into right behavior)—right relationships between God and us, others, and creation and being able to recognize when right relationship is not being shown. That recognition begins the pathway to just action in the world.

Just action requires our congregations to develop a just imagination. It requires us to be able to see like God sees, to see the vision that God has for all of creation, and then to begin to see how that vision can become reality in the lives of those around us.

The prophetic tradition invites us to expand such imagination. It gives us the patterns of the people of Israel (could we say the human patterns). These patterns begin with a sense of entitlement and self-centeredness. The people quickly become sure of their special relationship, of their chosen-ness. This leads to unfaithfulness as they quickly forget about the most vulnerable among them:

> *The LORD proclaims:*
> *For three crimes of Israel,*
> *   and for four, I won't hold back the punishment,*
> *because they have sold the innocent for silver,*
> *   and those in need for a pair of sandals.*
> *They crush the head of the poor into the dust of*
> *the earth,*
> *   and push the afflicted out of the way.*
> *(Amos 2:6-7a)*

Jesus and Justice

Jesus comes to the world in the midst of a deeply unjust situation for the most vulnerable in society, he being one of them. The powerful were becoming more powerful, the lowly more lowly. Jesus comes as a sign of who he comes to save and as Zechariah's song reminds us:

Because of our God's deep compassion,
 the dawn from heaven will break upon us,
 to give light to those who are sitting in darkness
 and in the shadow of death,
  to guide us on the path of peace.

(Luke 1:78-79)

Mary tells us that with Jesus' coming:

He has shown strength with his arm.
 He has scattered those with arrogant thoughts
 and proud inclinations.
 He has pulled the powerful down from their thrones
  and lifted up the lowly.
He has filled the hungry with good things
 and sent the rich away empty-handed.

(Luke 1:51-53)

From the very beginning, the ministry of Jesus showed us God's concern for justice as a key expression for the restoration of all of creation. Jesus heals and through healing frees and restores. Jesus frees those bound by demon possession and leprosy, both illnesses that made those afflicted broken from their society. Jesus raises the dead, feeds the hungry, and constantly reminds the religious leaders that they have forgotten their reason for being.

The most telling of all the stories of Jesus is his encounter with the rich young man. A man that was faithful to his religious tradition, a man that was good, a man that did most things right, but as Jesus said, "'There's one more thing. Sell everything you own and distribute the money to the poor. Then you will have treasure in heaven. And come, follow me.' When he heard these words, the man became sad because he was extremely rich" (Luke 18:22-23).

Restoration and justice begin with our own encounter with Jesus. Our hearts are longing for more, to be made right, to find healing and wholeness; this longing is brought forth by the Holy Spirit so that we can come to Jesus and hear words of freedom, of salvation, of being made right. As we grow justly we look around and instead of seeing only our own need, our own just life, our own holiness, we begin to also see the brokenness around us. We are awakened to the idea that God cares not just for those who claim to be part of the promise but truly for all of creation.

Because there is brokenness in the world, justice is needed. God is calling us to be agents of making right in the world, to smooth the rough edges of relationships around us and to be agents of reconciliation in the world.

Today there is still doubt, jealousy, evil and wickedness, there is unfaithfulness and tribalism. Today we find ourselves unable to hear, much less be in relationship with the other, unable to listen openly, unable to withhold judgement, assumption, and bias. Again and again injustice seems to prevail.

Communities of faith must root their lives in the story of our faith. This story calls us to a way of life that restores the shalom of God in the world. From the very beginning God has called a people to be a light to the nations. The church continues this call today. We remind each other as the baptized people of our duty and anointing to model what it is like to make things right in the world. This is what justice is about.

Unfortunately we have tended to see justice as a type of specific call related, yet separate, from our call of discipleship. When we look at Scripture this could not be further from the truth. It turns out that justice is an essential posture, the fruit of the growth of love in our souls. I believe part of the reason why this misunderstanding has emerged is because of the English language translation of the word *dikaiosyne* (justice) as "righteousness," a stiff and easily misunderstood way of rendering "making things right."

If we are the church, then we are a people called to justice. As God's people we need to begin to speak to one another about the things that we see around us that need to be made right, that need to be made whole. We need to help one another develop the ability to see like Jesus sees. Speaking about these things cannot just happen from the pulpit. In fact the church is at its best in its work of justice when we begin to help one another see brokenness and need for healing in the every day of life: like Jesus—finding the need as he walked, talked, met, and encountered.

We also need to get over our fear of not being capable since we'll never be perfect. Here is one of the things that I am learning about what it means to live into the marks of hope: as we live into them, hope grows, but also our own faithfulness grows, our own Christ-likeness grows, the Holy Spirit becoming more present in us as God's people and in our communities.

Justice as the Language of Hope

When we gather for worship we are familiar with the rhythms of greeting, prayers, Scripture readings, sermons, and sacraments. No matter what style of worship, we gather together and we have expectations of what will be said and what will be heard, what will be done and what we will be called to do. In some congregations the emphasis might be on inspiration and in others tradition. Do we hear a call to justice? Or what happens when justice is mentioned?

Experience has shown that where you are living in the United States and what the cultural center guiding your United Methodist identity is will have a big impact on how justice will be heard and acted upon. In many parts of our country it will be seen as suspect, as something other than from the gospel. It will be seen as political, maybe even secular.

When did the word *justice* begin to get a bad rap? When did it become separated from the fabric of the gospel? When did justice become something that the church did not encourage and act upon? These are only some of the questions as we continue our conversation on justice.

Justice is at the cornerstone of our call as people of God for it expresses a key aspect of God's nature. As Isaiah 40:14 tells us: "Whom did he consult for enlightenment? Who taught him the path of justice and knowledge and explained to him the way of understanding?"

God is just. God makes sure that no one is forgotten and calls us to do what is right. In the life, death, and resurrection of Jesus Christ we see what justice looks like in the flesh. We see Jesus healing, reconciling, welcoming, restoring, forgiving, and loving. Jesus "justifies," aligning the ragged edges of our created world, bringing together what was once separated and making right out of what has gone wrong.

Justice is salvation.

What I hope we are learning is that the work of justice is the natural fruit of and essential part of the call of discipleship: the call to holiness. For the people of God our set-apartness (holiness) is rooted in doing that which God has required. The more like God we become, the more justice we will practice in the world.

Justice Is Our Language

Each week we gather for worship to hear the good news. Each week we hear songs of praise, we pray, and we hear our story—God's story. Each week we are invited to hear what is right.

At Grace Community, my home base for life in God, we gather as a growingly diverse people. Every week we find ourselves with people around us that do not look like us, that do not have our story, nor our history. We are becoming increasingly aware of the many ways that we and the community around us fail to live into God's vision for us and for the world.

This point of view provides us a rich opportunity for practicing justice. We can look at our pew mates (row mates in our case since we have chairs not pews) and if we pay attention, we can come alongside them and together practice justice. We can hear their stories, heartbreaks, and the things that are keeping them from flourishing. We can also share our own life, our struggles, our questions, and our anxieties.

The community of faith provides us a perfect space to have conversations with our neighbors. Compassion, empathy, and hope allow room for us to share the "ragged edges" that are visible in our homes, neighborhoods, and city. In a culture of increasing polarization, just action includes modeling for our community what it looks like to find common ground as we together seek to "make things right," so that communities are flourishing.

In Shreveport, Louisiana, there seems to be a church on every corner. Yet injustice continues, hopelessness seems to be constantly right below the surface. This is made evident by what I would call the most obvious symptom of hopelessness: violence. In the last few years we have seen an increase in violent crime across our city. Some say that it is not an increase but that it is just more visible. Either way something is not right. If you peel the layers you will see that if we continue to have a growing gap in educational opportunities, workforce development, and affordable housing, we will continue to see the signs of hopelessness: increasing violence.

The church and a deeply churched community, a community where Christian religion runs deep and where Jesus is the subject of daily conversations, must find ways to imagine the possibilities for the practice of justice. What if we began to ask: How is God calling us to do what is right for our neighbor? How is God calling us to the common good?

We have the example in Jesus. Again and again we encounter him in the gospel telling stories, raising our awareness of our need for God and for each other. We sit in our churches week after week and hear the cycles of the story of Jesus. There are many churches, many people in those churches, and many opportunities to be reminded of the Christian story.

I often think about this during Advent. Each year we are given the Canticle of Mary as one of the lessons. In the churches that I have served over the years I've had the great joy of hearing my spouse sing Rory Cooney's "Canticle of the Turning," a beautiful arrangement of Mary's song:

> My heart shall sing of the day you bring.
> Let the fires of your justice burn.

In the lyric that follows, Cooney writes that our tears will be gone and a new dawn will follow. Even if we don't hear justice preached, we hear it read, sung, or prayed. God's people in our churches have a new opportunity each week to remember what God requires of us. This reminder should open our eyes, should awaken us, convict us, and more importantly should move us toward justice-making in the world.

Thursdays are busy days in the life of our congregation. Often I am making last minute adjustments before band practice. I can hear the voices outside my office as people gather around the building: yoga classes, recovery groups, scouts, and worship staff. As we continue our attempt to prepare for weekend worship, another part of our community gathers a few miles away.

The Common Ground Community is our missional partner in Cedar Grove, a economically depressed area of our city. This ministry is housed in a former United Methodist congregation. On Thursdays they too are very busy as they prepare for a community meal and food pantry time. A number of our folks are involved in this important ministry. They are practicing justice each and every time that they gather. They provide a small mark of hope as they come alongside community members and continue growing in their awareness of the many ways that the Cedar Grove community does not reflect God's desire for creation to flourish.

When we gather for worship on the weekend alongside our neighbors from Cedar Grove, the story of God screams of the need for justice. It is hard for us to ignore it if we have been part of the community meal, have tutored a child of poverty at the local elementary school, or have worked at the mobile clinic. These are only some of the many ways that I see justice bringing about a state of waiting among us—our Jesus conscience being prodded, bothered, and as I like to say, "messed with." Our eyesight being sharpened to the ways that justice is needed around us.

The many churches in our community are a reminder that we have the potential to be agents of the turning that God desires for us and for all of creation. We have this potential across denominational lines and ideological differences. In our communities, towns, and cities we have the opportunity to help each other, to challenge and influence each other to see like Jesus sees. Together we can make the kingdom known in both small and significant ways, showing others what it looks like to do what God requires.

Justice Is Re-Translation

At the beginning of this chapter I shared with you the importance of translation. I shared that translation is interpretation. It requires both knowledge of the two languages and understanding of the people, culture, and ways of life. As a seminary student in January of 2003, I had the great honor of traveling to Cuba with a group of faculty members to study Cuban language, culture, and religion. I went as both a fellow learner and one of the translators (interpreters) for the trip.

On the first Sunday morning of our trip we attended a local congregation for worship. The sanctuary was packed and there were people standing outside watching through the aluminum windows. That morning I had the honor to be the translator for Bishop Meadors, retired United Methodist bishop. He was asked by the Cuban pastor to address the congregation. I turned toward him and asked what he planned to say so that I could prepare. He said "I don't know I'll tell them what bishops say!"

As he stood before the congregation he began to greet them as a white, North American bishop would greet their people. I quickly realized that a word-for-word translation would not work. Instead I needed to interpret, in other words to greet them as a Caribbean Latino bishop would. The congregation responded with much joy. Bishop Meadors was thankful for their response and later said to me "I don't know what you told them, but it obviously worked!" I said, I told them what a bishop would!

In his book *Fin del Cristianismo Premoderno* (*End of Premodern Christianity*), Andrés Torres Queiruga tells us that in light of the changes in our world, the church must do the work of *retraducir*, of re-translating, the good news of Jesus Christ. God's people, especially religious leaders, must find ways to reconnect the story of God to today's people. This *retraducir* requires that we become students of the cultures where we live, work, and play. We must grow in our curiosity for the patterns of our neighbor's narratives, symbols, and ways of meaning-making.

In order for us to be faithful in our state of waiting, in *esperanza*, in hope, we must ask: What does flourishing sound like to the people around us at this time? What are the words, phrases, gestures, and facial expressions that best express what God requires (or best express justice)? How can we as the community of the baptized give people a picture, image, sign of what doing what God requires looks like?

Re-translation requires re-training, de-formation, and re-formation. This process begins in developing relationships with the natives. For me this means finding the people in our congregations and in our community who have a pulse for the new language, who are doing what God requires: healing, reconciling, freeing, and making broken things whole. These folks are around us, they might not be Christian, but obviously they are learning the language and are making a difference.

In Luke 9 the disciples are sent to be about the work of God's kingdom. Their work was so fruitful that the powerful took notice. Scripture tells us that the disciples were left "speechless" (verse 36) at what Jesus was doing. Soon their awe turned to pride

> *An argument arose among the disciples about who among them was the greatest. Aware of their deepest thoughts, Jesus took a little child and had the child stand beside him. Jesus said to his disciples, "Whoever welcomes this child in my name welcomes me. Whoever welcomes me, welcomes the one who sent me. Whoever is least among you all is the greatest."*

John replied, "Master, we saw someone throwing demons out in your name, and we tried to stop him because he isn't in our group of followers."

But Jesus replied, "Don't stop him, because whoever isn't against you is for you."

(Luke 9:46-50)

Like the disciples, we often fail to recognize the work of Jesus that is being done by those that we do not recognize. Re-translation requires that we pay attention and like Jesus see all restorative and freeing work as work that expresses the desire of God for the world.

This includes our willingness to work with others in our communities toward the common good. I can imagine connecting with other faith communities, local government, leaders in public education, and business leaders. Disciples of Jesus openly and with humility modeling our vision of God's kingdom while recognizing that as Jesus tells us "whoever isn't against" us is for us. If justice is going to flourish in our local communities, if all of our neighbors will experience the "state of waiting," it will happen only if we bring people together.

As disciples of Jesus, we must become justice makers in our every day life, coming alongside, building bridges, listening to the hurts, gathering people together, and acting with our communities in ways that make things right, that rehearse the kingdom of God.

With so many advances in social media we have an opportunity to broadly share stories of re-translation. Social media when used well can become this generation's sharing of testimony. At Grace Community we are learning the power of social networks to share what God is doing among us and in the world. This requires more than just an occasional post, it requires a decision to share both the victories and the lament, the places of flourishing and also the places of hurt.

Social media also gives us another opportunity. To model what it looks like to have different visions of the abundant life in Christ in ways that honor the other. Congregations that want to model justice as a mark of hope must also act justly (must do what God requires) in their engagement on social networks. How is our engagement in our congregational social networks and individual social networks a model of that which is just? What practices are needed to help us stay rooted in our identity in the midst of difficult interactions?

Finally congregations that are *hope-full* are reclaiming justice as the fruit of our commitment to love God, neighbor, and ourselves. Oscár Romero, archbishop of El Salvador and martyr, reminded us long ago that "true love means demanding what is just." In the midst of much turmoil in his native El Salvador, he called his people to remember that our claim to be a people of love meant that we had the duty to demand of those in power that they act justly. Demanding that the powerful act like Jesus, to act justly, was the cause for his assassination.

Romero's story reminds me, and it should remind all of us, that justice as a mark of hope means a willingness to be uncomfortable, unpopular, and a target. In my own pastoral ministry I have found that often the critics of just action begin by claiming that the pastor is being "political." After many years of struggle, I have come to realize that we have shaped our churches into seeing justice as merely a secular socio-political issue. We have missed many opportunities to preach what the scriptures tell us about justice, teach what the tradition tells us about justice, and lead congregations into what justice in our neighborhoods, workplaces, and cities look like in light of our faith in Jesus Christ.

I believe that this movement begins with reclaiming justice as the standard translation of the word δικαιοσύνη (*dikaiosyne*— justice). Imagine if our children, like I did as a child, hear the story of Scripture as the story of a God who calls us to participate in God's work of restoration, of making things right again, of flourishing. Try it for yourself, any time you encounter *righteousness* replace it with *justice*, see Matthew 3:14-15, 5:8-10, or 21:28-32.

This movement toward justice continues as we gather around table. Gathering to break bread and share cup, we remember. We remember the story of our faith, we remember our identity, we remember our primary calling as disciples of Jesus, we remember that this is not the end but only the beginning, we remember to become broken bread and poured cup. That only in our brokenness and our being poured out can we find wholeness again. Crazy, I know!

God from the very beginning has called us to justice. From the very beginning freedom, release, and healing have been part of our story. This has not been something that only some do (e.g,. social justice Christians), and it is certainly not something that only secular people worry about, but if we follow the biblical witness from Israel's history to wisdom literature, from prophetic texts to the story of Jesus, we are again and again called to the practice of justice as the result of our encounter with God.

Justice as a mark of hope becomes the fruit of our growth in love. This fruit opens our eyes to the world around us and to the ways that our communities, institutions, and way of life miss the mark, are broken, sick, and are in need of being made right. Preaching and discipleship with an eye toward justice means that we remind the community of our shared story and of our shared mission. Along the way we pay attention to those places around us:

our families, our neighborhoods, cities, and any place where life needs to be made right.

What You Can Do Today

In our Sunday school classes, small groups, and in worship we must reclaim being just as a key aspect of our Christ-likeness. We must recover our call to be in right relationship with God but also with neighbor, all neighbors, especially those that we would rather not have as neighbors. We must recognize that living a just life is living into holiness, being like Jesus, allowing God's image to be fully restored.

- Go to your Bible and every time that you see the word *righteousness* substitute the word *justice.*
- Read Mark's Gospel account and ask the questions: Where is Jesus? What happens when Jesus shows up?
- Gather with Sunday School teachers and ask how our children and youth are being shaped into a just people, into discipleship?
- Make your congregation a place that welcomes difference in every possible way.
- Speak to community leaders and ask for ways in which your congregation can be Jesus showing up.

Let us become re-translators of our biblical text and of the communities that we live in. We must read with an eye to God's vision for all creation. As we look around we must be willing to permit the Holy Spirit to continually convert us, allowing our heartbreak to turn into action and our communities into signs of our state of waiting for God to make all things right again.

Communion

I wonder when was the last time that you paid attention to the words we share and the actions we take part in when we gather for Holy Communion?

Before your next celebration of Holy Communion, open your hymnal, turn toward our services of Holy Communion, and read them from beginning to end. As you read, pay attention to the words that we say and the movements that the pastor and people are called to. Pay attention to how the story of our faith is told and how our ritual connects it to our discipleship today.

Who do we say God is?

What do we say God has done and is doing in Jesus?

What are we asking the Holy Spirit to do? What does it mean?

When we say "Amen" (may it be so), do we truly mean it?

Do we want for the Holy Spirit to make us what we have said, what we have affirmed?

As Mary McClintock Fulkerson and Marcia Mount Shoop remind us, "Eucharistic memory is about remembering Jesus' life, ministry, death, and resurrection for the sake of understanding how God is calling us to address the present context and its brokenness."[3]

Our present context and brokenness is often not "what God requires of us," it is not just. This is why we are gathered around Table again and again, to be reminded that the brokenness that we experience is not normative, that in Christ salvation, justice is possible. In some real ways the Eucharist provides us with the healing needed not just to be awakened but to begin doing the work of "doing what God requires."

The Eucharist is the medicine that allows us to develop a justice imagination. As we rehearse the story of salvation and are then given the presence of Christ we are empowered by the Spirit to become participants on behalf of God in shalom making, right making, justice practicing. Taking the bread and cup means re-commitment to our growth in love so that we can rehearse God's call to make things right, so that we claim that now we can indeed see like Jesus. Seeing, the kingdom imagination grows, allows us to behave, just behavior begins to make things right again, the kingdom of God coming near, the seeds of hope being born where they are needed most.

Communin Prayer

God who makes all things new.
You call us to do what you do,
to see what you see.
You remind us again and again
to be for others, what you
have been for us.

Letting judgment roll down like water,
Justice like an ever-flowing stream!

You created and continue creating,
When we failed,
you continued calling,
searching,
healing,
loving.

Letting judgment roll down like water,
Justice like an ever-flowing stream!

In Jesus
you showed us what
you looked like,

loved looked like
what restoration
and new creation looked like:
Hungry ones fed,
Naked ones clothed,
Lost ones found,
Poor ones lifted,
Rich ones humbled,
Possessed ones freed,
Sad ones comforted,
Confused ones directed,
Guilty ones forgiven,
Dead ones raised.

Letting judgment roll down like water,
Justice like an ever-flowing stream!

Pour out your Holy Spirit on us!
Pour out your Holy Spirit on these gifts!
Make them be for us the Body of Christ,
so that we can be the body of Christ,
redeemed, reconciled, restored, renewed,
the Body of Christ, doing what God does,
being who Jesus is,
the Body of Christ.

Letting judgment roll down like waters,
Justice Like an ever-flowing stream!

Chapter Four

THE (DIGITAL) WORLD IS MY PARISH

Matt Rawle

Technology doesn't have an opinion. People offer it [moral] value.

> —*Megan Smith, former chief technology officer of The United States of America, Games for Change Virtual Reality Summit 2017*

John Wesley said, "The world is my parish," but how does this apply when the world increasingly chooses to connect through social media over sanctuaries? What does evangelism look like in a digital world? Youth kickball tournaments are not nearly as popular as searching for Pokemon. Young professionals are streaming Bible studies on their lunch break rather than gathering for our Wednesday Night gatherings. People "check-in" on Facebook rather than sign the registration pad. You might think that trading paper for screens is an easy solution, but if you are a church leader and communicate church news only on Twitter, you will quickly discover the multitudes who have no idea what's going on because the newsletter no longer hits the mailbox.

The list of churches building websites is exponentially growing, and more congregations are moving to Facebook posts rather than mailers. The church is certainly moving into the information age, but there's a problem. The information age is all but over. Culturally, we are moving into the "augmented age," with self-driving cars, intuitive computers, and marketing that shows you what you want to purchase even before you've considered it. Are we to embrace this augmented reality, or stand firm as a countercultural icon of reality itself? Or are we somehow supposed to do both, like offering printed newsletters and e-mailed PDFs?

The 2017 Games for Change: Virtual Reality Summit, held in the summer of 2017 in New York City, offered a symposium of world-class speakers, presentations of cutting edge technologies, networking for industry leaders, and hands-on demos of the latest virtual reality projects hoping to find the right investor. Virtual Reality (VR) used to be a digital gimmick offering enhanced and immersive sight and sound to the two-dimensional screens of work and play. Over the last twenty years, VR has matured to accomplish more than surround sound and a 360 view. New technologies are able to achieve goals laboratory research and a flat screen could not produce. Now, virtual reality is changing reality itself. Instead of reading an MRI, we can put on goggles and see how the brain is working as if we were a synapse. Rather than talking about racial differences, we can virtually walk around in someone else's skin and feel how communities react to "the other." With an immersive blank canvas and a 3-D printer, we can manufacture what was thought to be impossible.

The Gospels offer a hint of innovation. One day Jesus was eating with his disciples and the Pharisees noticed that they had not washed their hands before dining. Jesus replies, "'Do you not see that whatever goes into a person from outside cannot defile, since it enters, not the heart but the stomach, and goes out into the sewer?' (Thus he declared all foods clean.) And he said, 'It is what comes out of a person that defiles'" (Mark 7:18-20 NRSV). Whether this was truly an innovative teaching or Jesus redefining what it means to be clean, this was certainly something new the Pharisees hadn't considered. Earlier in Mark's Gospel, Jesus is teaching in Capernaum. Four men carried their paralytic friend to seek healing from Jesus, but there were so many blocking the door that they could not pass through. They had to improvise, so they dug a hole in the roof and lowered the man down.

Improvisation is the root of innovation. Having to change direction and think through a problem from a different angle leads to innovative action. Ninety-nine bad ideas get you to the one that will change the world. Improvisation isn't about being clever or correct or entertaining; rather, improvisation is grounded in continuing God's story. Improvisation becomes innovation when we find the one idea that sticks. This isn't trial and error so much as it is knowing God's story so well that you can change and adapt the way it is shared without losing the story itself.

So what is the church's responsibility in sharing God's story in the midst of this cultural shift? Megan Smith, former chief technology officer of the United States and keynote speaker for the 2017 Games for Change Virtual Reality Summit, started the gathering saying by, "Technology doesn't have an opinion. People offer it [moral] value." Much like hope needs faith and love for a moral context, technology needs help. One of our jobs as Christians is to be the moral voice in the midst of new technologies. Instead of shying away from the augmented age, we must dive in to discover how the gospel message might be offered to a new generation.

Our Present Reality

Technology can be useful and isolating. My phone, television, and laptop are customized so that I can share photos, stories, and ideas with whomever I choose. The news hitting my notifications are from sources I prefer. These settings and filters are useful in helping me connect with people and sources I trust. Unfortunately, this also allows me to create a clearly defined barrier impermeable to new ideas, different cultures, and diversity of thought. This can create an echo chamber where anything outside of my preconceived ideas is suspicious, threatening, and to be feared.

Whether you consider yourself a traditionalist, progressive, centrist, or anything in between, we tend to gravitate toward like-mindedness. There's nothing wrong with communing with people who support similar values, mission, and goals. I don't feel you have to argue the other side of racism in order to be well rounded. The point is to recognize that the great technological segregation is not rooted in politics, theology, race, or creed; rather, technology puts us into only two categories—those who have access to it and those who do not.

One of the things in our Christian story that continues to capture me is that God put on flesh and walked among us in the person of Jesus. God entered into our world to breathe our same air, eat our food, walk the same streets, and sleep under the same starry sky. With the Incarnation (God in the flesh) as the centerpiece of the Christian message, you would think we would be experts in what it means to walk around in someone else's skin. Unfortunately, we seem adept at drawing lines in the sand and defining the other side rather than being confident enough in our convictions to put them aside long enough to listen to a differing point of view. Sometimes we forget that Jesus ate with sinners and the Pharisees, visited both sides of the Sea of Galilee, and worshiped at the temple where he overturned the money-changing tables. In other words, we really like our Jesus to be like us.

Some of the most interesting games at the Games for Change VR summit were games in which you could walk around in someone else's skin. One game offered you an experience to walk down the street as a different race. One of my friends noted after this experience that he was met with "eyes of suspicion" in the game, and this left him uneasy for all of the right reasons. Another game gave you the chance to walk alone in front of angry protestors. It doesn't matter what the protest is about. When you find yourself alone on the other side, the "flight or fight" response is almost overwhelming. These games were far from pleasant, but the uneasiness wasn't in the games themselves. The lump in your throat was the realization that the game you were playing is someone else's reality.

Therein lies our hope as The United Methodist Church. We have a vibrant history of being in ministry with those who do not have the resources to even purchase this book. Field preaching, fighting against child labor, lobbying for the disenfranchised, and lifting up those who have hit rock bottom have been part of our identity from the beginning, and it is what will tear down the silos into which we have segregated ourselves. Having the space and time to disagree over *The Book of Discipline* means that we know that we will eat tomorrow, our rent is paid, and the floodwaters aren't rising. It's not that poverty breeds agreement, but rarely have I heard the *Discipline* mentioned when mucking out a house after a hurricane.

Where We've Been

To get a feel for what this cultural and technological shift means, we need a brief history lesson. Humanity's identity as a culture-making people began while we were hunter/gatherers thousands of years ago. People would follow the herd, seek shelter in nearby dwellings, and use only what they needed. You almost get the sense that the biblical story about the man and the woman walking with God in the garden of Eden points to this era of human history, but life during this age was far from an idyllic garden. New technologies such as building a fire, fashioning spears, and language helped us to hunt and gather on the move.

Once humanity became efficient hunters and gatherers, we started ritualistic practices like burying our deceased and painting on cave walls. These ritualistic practices made staying in the same place a priority because location started to hold a significant cultural meaning. Our desire to honor place through monuments and markers led to the innovation of agriculture. In this era we find more permanent shelters, consistent nourishment, and defined borders. Many have suggested that the struggle between Cain and Abel in Genesis 4 details the struggle between hunters of a previous age and farmers on the cutting edge of technology. After Cain, the farmer, rose up against Abel, the shepherd, Cain fled to the east to build the first city mentioned in Scripture.

The agricultural age gave rise to technologies such as the plow, animal domestication, roads, and the wheel. Acquiring life's necessities became easier, and work became more individualized. Farmers, bankers, builders, and priests make up the new workforce. Egyptians built pyramids that touched the sky, Greeks pondered the meaning of life, Indians put numbers in their place with the Hindu-Arabic numeral system, and Romans conquered the Mediterranean. This is the age in which most of the Bible was recorded, which is why so many of Jesus' parables talk about vineyards, mustard seeds, money, and building on solid ground.

Even though staying in the same place is certainly more convenient than constantly roaming, not every community is self-sustaining. The agricultural age led us into the age of trade and exploration. Charting the stars while sailing the seas and standardizing language and numbers were necessary innovations for discovering far-off lands and trading goods. Interestingly, the previous ages lasted for thousands of years, but the age of trade and exploration lasted only a few hundred. Technology allowed innovation to happen exponentially, meaning that eras of human history were beginning to change faster than ever before.

After a few hundred years, rather than the thousands during the hunting/gathering and agricultural ages, there was another great cultural and technological shift. Once humanity started sharing goods over great distances, there was a desire to quickly and efficiently produce commodities, introducing the industrial age. Instead of living near farmland for food or a port for trade, we needed to live near factories. The industrial age made our cities swell, increased middle-class wealth, and created economies and governments built upon commodities itself. This age also necessitated a centralized market for goods and services. When you are on the clock, you can't go far for a lunch break. John Wesley realized this in the early eighteenth century.

Instead of opening the doors of the church to factory workers, hoping that they would come in, Wesley brought the church to the doors of the factory. His hope for spreading the gospel sent him to a new destination outside the walls of the church. This innovation within the Church of England brought the gospel to the poor and disenfranchised, offering them the hope of being heard and being valued.

Beginning in the mid- to late-twentieth century, about two hundred years after the industrial age began, the information age started to transform our centralized industrial way of living. With accessible transportation, telephones, and the Internet, the marketplace can be wherever we need it to be. You can connect with a friend, vendor, or business associate all from the same place. The church was slow in meeting this cultural shift. Arguably, mainline Protestants found themselves for the first time living in a new age with an old model. Industrial age-thinking necessitates lots of people all being in the same place. Instead of being a Christian at the coffee shop, your church would build one on its property.

Initially there was great success with large congregations taking root, sharing the gospel message through radio and television, but megachurches became increasingly few and far between. Eventually congregations began moving into the information age, taking advantage of e-mail, social media, online meetings, and digital databases. The only problem is, the church is still living in the information age, and the culture is shifting gears once again.

Where We Are

Several years ago a church member gifted me a second-generation iPad, which at the time was cutting-edge technology. I used the iPad in worship to read Scripture, to interact with the sanctuary screens, and to record attendance and giving. It seemed like a huge leap forward. Unfortunately, that second-generation iPad is all but obsolete. The operating system won't run the newest apps, and the charger needed to refuel the battery is no longer manufactured. So, I had to go back to bringing my Bible up to the pulpit. This wasn't a bad thing, but it made me keenly aware of how fast technology is progressing and constantly changing the way we gather with one another.

There can be resistance to new technologies from those within the church, but part of our calling as Christians is to be incarnational. We are to surround ourselves with our immediate culture in order to give it a new and holy meaning. God surrounded the divine with a less-than-divine first-century culture, in order to bring creation into communion with the creator. We sometimes make the mistake of thinking that innovation and technology are intrinsically counter to the gospel, but we are to be imitators of Christ, not imitators of the first century.

Today we are venturing into uncharted territory, and change is happening quickly. The hunting-gathering age lasted thousands of years, but the information age was barely around for a few decades. This new augmented age into which we are living doesn't make connecting with a vendor easier, it makes connecting with a vendor unnecessary. Instead of programming computers to do what we need them to do, software is becoming intuitive, often telling *us* what we need before we know we need it.

So what does the church look like in this new age? Self-driving cars, algorithms, and intuitive machines will have an unprecedented effect on the way we connect with one another. In general, many congregations are still wrestling with the change from industrial to information age. For example, the mega church explosion of the last twenty years fits well within the industrial age where everything you need is in one place (think coffee shop in the narthex, basketball gym, sign-up clipboards at the welcome station), but the world was moving on to the information age. Churches are just now entering into the information age (Facebook pages, websites, online registration for Vacation Bible school) while many outside of the church are blazing a new trail. In what ways will the church be left behind when technology is changing as rapidly as the church is moving slowly?

On the one hand, the way we gather as communities of faith will need to look different. Think of the way you register attendance on Sunday morning. Most churches pass out registration pads during the service for people to sign their name, offer prayer requests, and request a pastoral visit. This is industrial age thinking, meaning that for this to work, you need everyone in the same place at the same time. (Is it worth mentioning the human contact aspect here? Knowing whom you're with?) Some churches are moving into the information age with automatic check-in through wireless systems and RFID keychains or Facebook check-ins. Folks can come and go on campus at different times, and their information will be recorded. Could it be that in the augmented age, our pastoral software will be so intuitive it will suggest a pastoral visit even before congregants had thought to ask for one?

On the other hand, some things in the church won't change and don't need to change. Computers will always excel in precision, repetition, and exchanging information. People will always have the upper hand when it comes to ethics and moral expression. Maybe the church's role in the augmented age is to offer a consistent moral compass in the midst of whatever technology has in store. The church cannot compete with Amazon in terms of digital footprint, but we can offer a prophetic voice when that footprint values profit over the people. We can certainly make strides in speeding up the Sunday morning registration process (information age), or skip it all together (augmented age), but our focus should always be on the names themselves rather than how they are collected.

A Future Without Fear

Over the last few months my daughter and I have been playing through the latest title in The Legend of Zelda video game franchise called *Breath of the Wild*. The game developers created a deeply detailed world map in which there are few places you can't go. You can play the game in whatever order you want. You can follow the story, incrementally developing your skill and items to defeat monsters with increasing difficulty, or you can test your luck and immediately fight Gannon, the baddest monster of them all. There's something liberating when playing a game that allows you to go almost anywhere at any time in the world map. You kind of have to figure it out as you go. While you play a story emerges. Villagers ask you to go to the mountain, a sage points you to a garden, and monsters force you to develop certain sword techniques. If you play the game according to the narrative of the unfolding story, you will likely be more successful in your adventure, but playing by the rules isn't necessary.

Jesus never let the rules get in the way of doing God's work. It's not that Jesus broke the rules or ignored God's narrative that had been shared throughout Israel's history; rather, Jesus followed the story, went to the mountain, prayed in the garden, and resisted a monster's temptation so that the story could be fulfilled. In a way, like playing *Breath of the Wild*, once you've completed a quest, you don't have to do it again. You certainly can play a completed quest, but there's nothing gained by it. It has served its purpose, and you are free to continue the journey forever changed. Jesus came to fulfill the law so its purpose would be complete. You can certainly live as if the law is God's final word, but it would be as if Christ died for nothing (Galatians 2:21).

One of my favorite features of this game, or almost any game for that matter, is the "save" function. If you happen to fail in a quest and your character dies, you simply start over. No matter how difficult, treacherous, or impossible the game becomes, your progress is never lost. There's no penalty for failure. In fact, the game encourages failure. The more you fail, the more you learn about your limitations, and the more you learn about your limitations, the more you dive into the game. For example, The Legend of Zelda has always been a game of hearts. You always start the game with three hearts. When you take damage or get injured, you lose a portion of your hearts. You quickly realize that you can't get very far in the game with so few hearts. So, you begin what's called "side quests" in order to gain additional hearts. To keep these hearts replenished, you have to forage for ingredients to cook meals. Ingredients combined in different ways offer different abilities. Just after the opening scene, you could go directly to the castle, and try to defeat the boss with your limited hearts, but this isn't much of a game. In other words, your failures early in the game actually make the game more interesting, immersive, and fun to play.

There's no penalty for failing, and this lack of penalty offers a lack of fear. Some of the first words spoken at the tomb after Jesus was resurrected was, "Be not afraid." Certainly the angels offered peace to the women at the tomb because this never-before-seen Resurrection leaves us with lots of questions, but more to the point, having no fear is what the Resurrection is all about. When death no longer has the final word, there is nothing in all of creation we should fear. No matter the obstacles or monsters or seemingly impossible quests, God's "save" feature, the prevenient, justifying, and sanctifying grace offered to us through Father, Son, and Spirit, is always with us.

As John Wesley often noted,[1] this grace is resistible. The save feature in *Breath of the Wild* means little if you give up, turn the game off, and refuse to play. It seems that the church is so fearful of failing that we would rather turn the game off than see into what adventures our failures will lead, or with little heart, we would rather head straight to the boss. This is why Jesus' ministry didn't end with his baptism. Rather than come up from the waters of baptism and head straight to Jerusalem and the cross, Jesus seemed to meander. He grew in wisdom, healed the blind, offered parables and teachings, went back and forth from village to mountain, rich and poor, and Jew and Gentile. Maybe it's time for the church to meander in the wilderness with ears tuned to God's voice and the experience of our sisters and brothers rather than seek easy answers to preserve what we think we are called to protect.

What Can You Do Today?

It is amazing to see how human innovation is stretching the definition of what we think is possible. Virtual Reality has the capability to immerse us in a reality outside of our small, individual, and subjective points of view. We can digitally walk around in someone else's skin with the help of a computer and a headset. Walking around in someone else's skin is the cornerstone of the Christian faith. God put on flesh to show us the reality of the kingdom of God, a place where the poor are welcomed, the mournful are comforted, and the hungry are filled. We do not innovate just to create a new social media app or be the first to go to Mars. This is neither our calling nor commission. Our role is to ensure that our technological advances are always tethered to a Christ-centered ethic. So how do we live into that role?

- **Be a fish out of water.** Get familiar with a new technology. Maybe download a prayer reminder app, or read about new developments in transportation. Then, think about how this technology might bring us into communion with God and each other.

- **Be imitators of Christ, not the first century.** It's less important to keep traditions as it is to communicate what traditions mean to the next generation. For example, keeping the twenty-year tradition of a living nativity is less important than communicating the Christmas story itself.
- **Be strong enough to fail.** Risk using a new technology in your faith community.
  - o It could be as simple starting a church Snapchat account.
  - o Donate new computers to the local public school so that all in your community have easy access to technology.
- **Break down the echo chamber.** Be sure that the work you do for Christ is not only for those with access to e-mail, text reminders, and website driving directions. Try communicating an event only by word of mouth and see who shows up.

Holy Communion in the Augmented Age

Not long ago I had the chance to meet with a United Methodist elder who was considering changing order to become a deacon. For a long time he struggled with this change because he loved officiating at the Lord's Table during Holy Communion. Affirming his decision was a revelation about what his role at the Table was supposed to be. He said, "Although I won't preside at the Table, it's my job to get people there." In other words, whether we gather with iPads or hymnals, online or in person, the point for him was bridging the gap between where the bread is broken and the souls who need it most.

Does this mean that there should be a countercultural element in the church against the fast-paced technological revolution?

Should the church jump headfirst into a world of zeros and ones? Should we have one foot in each world, like bringing your printed Bible to worship even though the scripture is on the screens? Maybe this is the true beauty of Communion. The broken bread and the cup outpoured point us to Jesus who was incarnate—fully divine and fully human. Whether the Communion song is on the screens or sung by a choir, the bread still has to be placed in the hands of those who can't put down their smartphones and the hands of those who might never hold the latest gadget.

Communion Litany

As we gather around the table we remember God,
Author of innovation and inspiration,
Who unceasingly seeks to be with us,
In our newsfeeds and screens,
Weaving through 140 characters and beyond,
Deliver us from being tethered
To what we claim is wireless.

With your people on earth, and all the company of heaven
We praise your name and join in their unending hymn:

Holy, holy, holy, Lord, God of power and might,
Heaven and earth are full of your glory.
Hosanna in the highest!
Blessed is the one who comes in the name of the Lord
Hosanna in the highest!

Holy are you, and blessed is your Son, Jesus Christ
Who put on flesh and walked among us
Surrounding himself with our culture
In order to give it a new, holy, and redeemed meaning

He took bread, made with human hands,
   And with his hands he broke it, saying,
      This is my body, broken for you.
After supper, he took wine,
   Pressed from grapes cultivated through invention and
   innovation,
      Offered it to the disciples and said,
         This is my blood poured out for you.
When we break the bread and receive the cup we remember Christ,
   re-member the body of Christ,
   and proclaim the mystery of faith:

Christ has died, Christ is risen, Christ will come again.

Pour out your Holy Spirit on us gathered here,
   And on these gifts of bread and wine
Help us to live without fear or division
   That we might share your grace,
      By thought, word, and deed,
      By screen, phone, or software
With our sisters and brothers across the world,
   And those standing next to us,
      Or against us,
      Or in spite of us.

Through your Son, Jesus Christ,
   With the Holy Spirit, in your holy church
   All honor and glory is yours, Almighty God,
      Now and forever. Amen.

Chapter Five
TOGETHER WE RISE

Katie McKay Simpson

Hope is a song in a weary throat.
—From the poem "Dark Testament"
The Rev. Pauli Murray, rights activist and priest

I was offering a lecture at my local university in a women's history series called "Trouble and Hope for Today's Women in Ministry." There was a young woman I have talked with from time to time on campus who had fallen out of relationship with the church of her birth who raised her hand and asked me a question. I called on her, and she asked me, "Why would you believe in and preach from a holy text that largely lifts up the stories that are so cruel to women? Where is the hope in that?" I have often been asked why I lend myself to the work of guarding a tradition that so freely discriminates against women and reflects a culture few would ever want to emulate today.

There is no doubt that the Bible was written in a time when women were not valued. Because of that, men are named significantly more often, men serve as protagonists in the biblical stories more often, and men hold positions of leadership more often. In addition, there are stories and laws found in Scripture regarding women that show a profound inequality as it relates to the way societies viewed women. These are the stories surrounding women like Hagar, Dinah, Tamar, Jephthah's daughter, and so on revealing the inequity that characterized day-to-day life for women living in biblical times.

But still, it's astounding that in the midst of such a culture, so many women were called out by God as leaders and teachers in their communities throughout Scripture. When the Holy Spirit descended upon the first Christians at Pentecost, Peter drew from the words of the prophet Joel to describe what had happened, saying, "Your sons and daughters will prophesy . . . Even on my servants, men and women, I will pour out my Spirit in those day" (Acts 2:17-18). The breaking in of the new creation after Christ's resurrection unleashed a host of new prophetic voices. While some may try to downplay biblical examples of female disciples, deacons, leaders, and apostles, no one can deny the Bible's long tradition of prophetic vision and leadership by women—from Deborah, Miriam, Huldah, Esther, Junia, Phoebe, Priscilla, Chloe, Tabitha, Mary, Martha, Nympha, Lydia, and the other unnamed women who were judges, prophetesses, apostles, and evangelists. I believe this prophetic vision is as important today—perhaps even more important—as it was in the days of the early church.

I remember attending the United Methodist clergywomen's gathering in Houston just last year. We kicked off Monday evening with a procession of women clergy from around the world and a worship service in which the question was asked, "Are we still seeking crumbs from Jesus?" It was the story of the Canaanite woman whose father said she was demon-possessed. She kept calling after Jesus, and the Scripture reads:

> *Jesus did not answer a word. So his disciples came to him and urged him, "Send her away, for she keeps crying out after us."*
>
> *He answered, "I was sent only to the lost sheep of Israel."*
>
> *The woman came and knelt before him. "Lord, help me!" she said.*
>
> *He replied, "It is not right to take the children's bread and toss it to the dogs."*
>
> *"Yes it is, Lord," she said. "Even the dogs eat the crumbs that fall from their master's table."*
>
> *Then Jesus said to her, "Woman, you have great faith! Your request is granted." And her daughter was healed at that moment.*
>
> (Matthew 15:23-28 NIV)

To the young woman attending the lecture who asked me that very important question, I said, "It is true that there is a healing that needs to happen in our church for women to truly thrive to the level of their God-bestowed giftedness rather than settling for the crumbs that are thrown our way. There is also a deep need for gifted women of every generation to seek healing so that we ourselves may move forward constructively and unafraid rather than looking to the past in bitterness. Both are needed so that gifted women can truly claim our place in God's vision for transforming the world. That's why I stay. There's more than a lifetime work to be done."

Our Present Reality

The United Methodist Church's unity is threatened today. In this moment of uncertainty about our future together, we have the responsibility to lift up our very best leaders in a time when we need our most effective and faithful minds and hearts working toward a solution for the future of The United Methodist Church. This denominational division is, on the surface, centered around the differences we find among our global church related to one important theological conversation on human sexuality. I would suggest that this theological impasse that has deep ramifications for real people in our church is only the presenting concern. There are even deeper forces at work that have brought us to our place of decline, institutional sickness, and structural anxiety that are so prevalent at every level of the church today.

This growing division has revealed an awareness that many on the margins have seen and known, but others are only now coming to discover. The structure of privilege many leaders in our church have come to take for granted (and others on the margins have learned to navigate and/or tolerate) is being directly challenged, deconstructed, and reconstituted at an accelerating rate. We have always celebrated and continue to celebrate that faithful, called men can and should lead in God's church. However, with each expansion of clergy and lay leadership to voices that enable more diverse gender identities and ethnic backgrounds to claim a "seat at the table" of leadership, a displacement, or reseating if you will, naturally occurs. It has become a fight for access, authority, and genuine appreciation and acceptance of "the other."

Within our fractured communion, the reality we face is that the average age of clergy is in the late fifties and rising. These clergy and committed laypeople in the boomer generation are reaching retirement age, and the rate of clergy retirement in our various annual and central Conferences is growing exponentially. All the while, if seminary enrollments are any indication, over 50 percent of seminary students in many Methodist-related seminaries are women, and vacant pulpits create spaces opening for a more widely diverse young clergy base to lead and serve formidably in the present age. There is great need to share the gospel in a rapidly changing world. This is a time where we need every capable leader to be prepared, equipped, and empowered to reach our mission field for the sake of Jesus Christ now more than ever.

In their most recent study, "The State of Pastors," the Barna Group noted that the nomination of the first woman as her party's candidate for president of the United States was symbolic of the immense social shift made in the status of women in the United States over the past fifty years. A similar shift has been seen in women in CEO roles, those successfully launching new businesses, and ministerial roles in the United States, where women have steadily increased in their status and numbers in the church, particularly the mainline church.

We are grappling with what this shift will mean for women—and by virtue of our struggle, other marginalized persons as well—to have an equal seat at the table. Churches often mirror society's slowness to allow the decisions we make to become fully vested into the culture of who we are and what we do. To have our ideals meet in practice takes a considerable amount of time, and by virtue of the numbers and statistical evidence below, we still have a long way to go.

The State of Women in the Church

The number of women answering the call to ministry in clergy and lay service is exponentially on the rise these days. Barna reports that one in eleven Protestant senior pastors is a woman, which is triple the percentage of twenty-five years ago. Most of these women serve in mainline denominations, with virtually all mainline denominations (99%) ordaining women. However, it is sobering to consider that only 35% of non-mainline denominations permit women to hold senior or executive pastor roles. In comparison, The United Methodist Church reported 10.6% of clergy were female twenty-three years ago[1] compared with 27% in 2015, approximating the growth seen by Barna. In my annual conference, for instance, when I became an elder eleven years ago, there were only twelve women under the age of forty. Today, in 2017, the amount has almost tripled in size at thirty-five.

As a result, our assumptions about what effective leadership looks like in the pulpit and the pew is transforming before our eyes—and that change is great news for God's church! Expanding seats at the table, allowing for and advocating for other voices to join in the conversation allow for greater creativity, innovation, power, collaboration, vulnerability, and joy. This movement of raising up new, diverse, and capable leadership brings God glory and breaks the narrative that formidable opportunities for missional leadership are scarce and reserved for a select few. Our church is beginning to understand that our future growth is bound in commitment to seeing all rise to answer a call and in seizing the chance to equip them for reaching their deepest giftedness and potential. We are being reminded once again that effective, Spirit-led leadership—no matter the gender of the person—is generative.

It naturally expands opportunities to explore and act upon God's vision for our common future as we share the gospel story.

We must, however, approach this consideration of gender with utmost honesty about our present reality This mark of hope is, arguably, the most complicated because there is still much in the realm of women's leadership in the church that is not hopeful news. Consider some of these present realities that continue to plague our communion together:

In 2014, of the 177 United Methodist churches that had more than one thousand people on an average Sunday morning, only four had female senior pastors (and this number shrunk to three when one was elected to the episcopacy in 2016).[2] This reality among many points to one of the most important frontiers that we must address as a church: the disparity in gender representation in appointment-making and its relationship to pay differences. New national data reveals that female clergy earn 76 cents for each dollar earned by male clergy. This is substantially worse than the national pay gap of 83 cents. The clergy pay gap is even more stark when compared to similar occupations. Up until the year of this particular survey, national data on the clergy pay gap was unavailable.[3] According to the Bureau of Labor Statistics, in 2014 male clergy earned $1,007 per week; female clergy earned only $763. This is a $12,000 difference in annual earnings. In one of our annual conferences in the continental United States, a United Methodist bishop reported that "In 2015, the average cash compensation of the 30 highest paid female senior pastors was $47,910, while the average for the 30 highest paid male senior pastors was $73,336."[4] In the Virginia Annual Conference, some women earned up to $10,000 less than their male counterparts who had the same amount of experience. In both conferences, differences in salary increased with years of service.[5] When assessing the salaries of women following pastorates served in my own conference, I was heartened to see that the salaries from one person to the other did not change; however, their pastorates at these larger churches were shorter, if they were given the opportunity to be appointed to larger churches at all. For women of color, the picture related to compensation is even more dismal.

Lay women's leadership is also holding steady, and in some cases, declining at a time when leadership should continue to expand in annual conferences and on the general church level. General Conference women's delegate growth, for instance, was on the rise in the early 2000s, but lost ground in 2012 and 2016.

In the wake of these continuing challenges, there has been a revival of commitment and resilience emerging. We can see it in retention rates of our clergywomen: at the turn of the century, women were leaving local church ministry at a 10 percent higher rate than male clergy. As of 2012, in a survey of clergywomen remaining in ministry in the continental United States, there were 96 percent (previously 73 percent) of clergywomen in local church ministry in the North Central region, 97 percent (previously 69 percent) in the Northeastern, 96 percent (previously 75 percent) in the Western, 95 percent (previously 64 percent) in the South Central, and 98 percent (previously 67 percent) in the Southeastern. In general, all regions show about 20 percent to 30 percent of growth for clergywomen's participation in local church ministry.[6]

Maybe that's a witness to hope in its strongest form. It's easy to be joy-filled and courageous when there is nothing to fear, fight against, or lament. However, choosing to show up daily and continue to hold a posture of hope despite our present circumstances is a courageous act of trust that God's action will surely continue to pave the way.

Rising Hope

Even considering these realities, here are some of the places where I find hope rising in The United Methodist Church as we consider this complex topic of gender and leadership in the church.

Women's Leadership as an Asset to the Church

First, there is an increasing acceptance of women's leadership as an asset, not just a token responsibility, for any organization. According to Harvard Business Review, leaders of various companies interviewed realized that any solutions involving only 50 percent of the human population are likely to have limited success. Companies with female board representation have been found to outperform those with no women on their boards. Gender parity has been found to correlate with increased sales revenue, more customers, and greater relative profits. Companies in the top quartile for gender diversity were found to be 15 percent more likely to outperform those in the bottom quartile.[7]

One of the greatest barriers to women's promotion in church leadership has been a scrutiny that our leadership is not the kind needed for a program or corporate-sized church—that pastoral leaders must be more autocratic than most women characteristically are in the congregation. In the past, this assumption about the leadership profile that is expected in churches may have been common, but the leadership traits women possess, or the ones that we strive to develop, are not necessarily different or any more or less effective from those of our faithful male colleagues. They are just perceived and described with an often unaware gender bias. For instance, a strong administrative pastor that manages the gifts of staff and lay volunteers (and just happens to be male) often is described as a strong leader with clear vision and commitment to accountability for the sake of our gospel witness. Women—myself and others I've known—who exhibit these same traits are sometimes described as "high maintenance and rarely able to be pleased."

Our perception of women is becoming more multidimensional, and that shift has been and will continue to become a gift to the church. The entire church is growing to recognize the unique abilities of many of our women—an ability to see and value both the small and big picture (people and systems), organization, emotional intelligence, and vision-casting to name a few. I find hope in the possibility that in the future, there will be no male or female leaders, but leaders period, each with their own set of unique gifts to offer at the table.

We see the rise of relational, collaborative leadership being praised in business circles that—mind you—are still dominated by men. The study on gender diversity by Marcus Noland, Tyler Moran, and Barbara Kotschwar for the Peterson Institute for International Economics says there is a positive correlation between the presence of women in corporate leadership and performance in a magnitude that is not small.[8] It is hard to nail down the exact performance bump a woman's presence can lend a company—only about half of the companies studied had any female leaders at all. But the study did suggest that having a woman in an executive position leads to better performance, with the more women the better. The study points out that diversity in general probably leads to higher performance. A single female CEO doesn't perform better than her male counterpart. However, when controlling for gender in the rest of the company, a higher rate of diversity throughout the organization has an impact, the study found. The Peterson Institute study is one of the largest on gender diversity, as it looked at 21,980 firms in ninety-one countries.

In the last few years, circles of entrepreneurs are appreciating and, in fact, adopting a shift from autocratic leadership styles to more collaborative styles as the primary approach for effectiveness in visionary leadership and management. I remember walking into a coworking space in Dallas started by White Rock UMC called "The Mix Coworking & Creative Space." There is an emerging awareness that the Spirit works in the collective. Examples like this show that no pastor should have the audacity to believe that she or he can come to wisdom of the Spirit for a church's future only on his or her own terms. It is not the way of the gospel. This signals a strong possibility for those of all genders, particularly women, to move away from apology for who we are to claiming the formidable contribution of gifts and perspective we bring to the table.

Women Supporting Women

A mark of hope identified and emerging only in recent years is women supporting each other—one where women even at the highest levels of leadership in our church are finally supporting other women, mainly because we finally trust that there is enough opportunity to go around. One of the saddest parts about the resistance to women is that the very allies we assume would support us have, in the past, held us back—resistance often comes from other women. We see this dynamic in politics and the executive boardrooms of business, right down to the dynamics of our own friends and family. This is a reality that exists because the fear and anxiety around a lack of opportunity has been so high.

Until now, being a woman in ministry was often described as a fairly isolating experience. Rev. Carole Cotton Winn, one of the matriarchs of clergywomen in our conference and the first female district superintendent in Louisiana, described it this way:

"There was a profound sense of isolation I experienced as a woman coming into ministry. Pair this with getting dropped into a local church—alone, in churches with no staff or minimal staff while many of us often still single. In those days, we would gather once a year in the center of the state and could all fit comfortably in a cabin in the woods. The group was mostly all white, but over the years it became a rich diversity. It was those annual retreats in which we found community. They were both life giving and life-saving in the early years of women in ministry."[9]

Women were first ordained in 1956, but it took a couple of decades for women in The United Methodist Church to be able to receive appointments in any local congregation. Generally, in the South Central and Southeastern Jurisdictions of the United States, the climate was so adversarial to having a non-male leader in the pulpit every Sunday, women often worked in extension ministry or, in the best cases, associate roles on church staffs.

This attitude began to change, and as the first women became judicatory leaders in various jurisdictions in the 1980s, the 90s and early 2000s brought opportunities for women to take on greater leadership in the local church. However, the old adage "there's only room for one" seemed to prevail as the assumption of the day. Usually there would be only one place for a woman on a cabinet, a College of Bishops, or a larger pulpit in an annual conference. It was an isolating experience for the women who rose into these positions, as well as for the others that still struggled to find their own opportunity and place to serve.

A hopeful turn lately is that there are more than enough opportunities and spaces to go around. (However, they may not always be in the positions at the highest levels of influence—yet.) God is healing our wounds, fortifying us to speak boldly and with renewed resolve, paving a way forward, and changing the frame of our sight to hold a more abundant view for what is possible through the spiritual leadership of our churches. This God-empowered abundance in our systems is beginning to set women (and all people) free to be less isolated, less fearful about the prospects of their lifelong ministries, and more willing to help each other succeed.

In the places and times where women don't receive the mentorship that they need to rise into places of formidable leadership in the church, we seem to be creating these spaces ourselves. In my annual onference, for instance, we have begun what is called a Young Clergywomen's Cohort—a grassroots effort of clergywomen under forty who gather twice a year for mutual learning, coaching, and accountability. These women are identifying the agency they have to fill in the gaps in their learning and experience and invite others to share what they know for everyone's benefit so that all move forward in personal sanctification and deeper leadership effectiveness together.

We must continue this trend, and to do so The United Methodist Church must not rely on women to simply fill in the gaps of their experience through their own initiative. This commitment must grow even wider at the highest levels of our polity and practice. We must commit to look more closely at our appointment system in light of the impact on all women, particularly racial-ethnic women. The church still struggles with institutional racism, sexism, work-family stress that affects women disproportionately, and the "economic stratification" within the United Methodist clergy system. This is something we have to painfully, but directly address in each of our mission fields.

Our church is beginning to grasp the gospel call we all are encouraged to adopt through the witness of Holy Scripture—that we will not reach our God-given potential until we *all* reach our God-given potential together.

Holding the Church Accountable for Sexual Harassment and Abuse

We live in a culture today that has a deplorable tolerance of sexual abuse and assault against the vulnerable. It is alive and well in the highest offices in the world's political stage, to recent stories of actors and producers in Hollywood, to pastors in our pulpits and lay folks in our congregations. Because women have begun to speak with holy boldness against these violations of their own security on their own accord, or through collective campaigns like the recent social media effort #metoo, awareness and accountability have grown for the church. We are reminded now more than ever that we are called to become a body that is a safe place for the vulnerable, speaks truth to power, and is purified to witness in a refreshed, trust-filled way to a deeply hurting world.

With the rise of women in leadership, we have found that there is a greater impatience and critical eye toward those that would test the boundaries of verbal and physical abuse simply because there has, in some cases, been a lack of accountability and response in the past. I find that today, as more women and men are being freed with the permission to question and speak out about their experiences, there is renewed hope in the questioning.

There is hope—that victims who express that they have been violated will be believed; that with every story told, light will be shed, and others that come behind will be protected from harm. We can find that across the connection, violence against women is diminishing, though not completely. There has been an encouraging rise in sexual harassment training and focus on upholding standards on clergy boundaries in most annual conferences. We are aware that a lack of attention to this can have dire consequences. Violence, abuse, and harassment is being checked, more safe spaces are being created, and God's church is being restored. Through stories in the news daily, we are reminded that it only takes one predator in a local church to perpetrate unimaginable pain—one person with no boundaries. And in it all, the church—our church—wears the wound.

So we find that where women in church leadership have had to swallow their pride and keep truth hidden when verbal or physical boundaries have been broken, now space is being made and encouraged for those truths to come out in the open. On blogs and social media private groups for United Methodist clergywomen, we continue to see both signs of advocacy in our churches and difficult signs that verbal abuse and physical intimidation are still very much alive. But we are leaning on each other and not falling silent to that which taints the trust our people have in our congregational leadership. This movement, as it continues, will prepare the Body of Christ to continue to grow in God's grace, being purified to receive the most vulnerable for renewed health, abundant life, and healing that lasts.

Years ago, I was sitting in a room with clergywomen ranging from twenty-five to seventy-plus years old. We were women with vastly different perspectives around hope as it pertains to clergywomen's celebration, acceptance, safety, opportunity, and proven advancement in the church. As it is with any shifts in generational experiences, one group paves the way, another normalizes, and still a third reaps the benefits. I am able to serve today in a more secure environment because others—women primarily—spoke up against injustice before me. In cabinet rooms, Boards of Ordained Ministry, on Staff-Parish Relations Committees, and in the pulpit, I see the world around us becoming more mindful of our complicity related to these issues and less disposed to allow sexist attitudes to go unchecked. This is all, primarily, because women and their allies have held on to an unwavering hope, demanding respect for themselves by the power of God. I continue to try in every way possible to speak against and ward against other abuses for those women that will serve and follow in my pastorates.

Deepening Commitment of Male Allies

One of the most hopeful places God's movement seems to be is the openness of male allies to expand opportunities for women to be mentored and to lead. Especially as it relates to having experience in senior and executive pastoral leadership in larger congregations, we cannot only rely on women to mentor women. These antiquated, gender-based boundaries hold women back from learning directly from our best spiritual and administrative leaders, especially in annual conferences that may have few women, or none at all, who have been appointed into those roles.

Harvard Business Review wrote recently on what is commonly known as "The Billy Graham Rule"—an encouragement for male leaders of faith to avoid spending time alone with women to whom they are not married. This means not only meetings but also meals, travel, and attending conferences where important conversations for learning, development, and strategy for an organization often occur. The expressed reason given is to protect his reputation by warding against either falling prey to sexual temptation or inviting gossip about impropriety.

As a married clergywoman, I   have standards about my conversations and connections with male laity and clergy colleagues—often meeting only in public places or in rooms with cracked doors or a window for visibility. This practice is as much for transparency on my part as it is creating a safe, unconfined space for conversation with colleagues or counseling with laypeople. But this Billy Graham "rule" rises from a different place and continues to relegate women away from key conversations in which they could not only learn but also formidably contribute. This standard has high moral intentions, but is a rule based primarily out of fear rather than morality. The authors of the article, both men in the business world, in their commentary say,

> Although thoughtful professional boundaries create the bedrock for trust, collegiality, and the kind of nonsexual intimacy that undergirds the best mentoring relationships, fear-based boundaries are different. By reducing or even eliminating cross-sex social contact, sex segregation prevents the very exposure that reduces anxiety and builds trust . . . The preservation of men and the exclusion of women from leadership roles will be perpetuated everywhere that the Billy Graham rule is practiced.[10]

The authors also remind us that Jesus himself was known to meet alone with women (e.g., the Samaritan woman at the well). As we continue to move toward Christian perfection, we follow the model of Christ for whom showing attention, hospitality, compassion, and elevating the dignity of women everywhere he encountered them was more important than any threat of gossip. Our leaders should have the courage, for the sake of the health and wholeness of God's church, to leave this well-meaning, but antiquated standard behind.

I have been an elder since 2007 in The United Methodist Church, and in eight years of associate and executive pastor roles before my present appointment, I served in ministry with six male senior pastors. That experience of having many different models of mentoring or watching my colleague choosing not to take the opportunity to develop and mentor in a male-female partnership was invaluable to my formation as a pastor. It gave me a deeper awareness of how women in second-chair roles have the potential to be prepared by their senior leaders to take on formidable senior and solo roles of leading churches themselves, but that potential still is not often realized. I continue to be thankful for men who are in senior leadership, district superintendents, and for friends who are contemporaries (like my fellow authors Matt Rawle and Juan Carlos Huertas) who understand that when women succeed, those of all genders succeed alongside them. There are many church leaders out there who have boldly begun to see a wider vision for God's church, and actively advocate alongside women in the church for it—seeking to mentor women in the workplace and involve them, even make space for them, in key projects for learning, development, and eventual success.

I am mindful, however, that my particular experience has not been the norm everywhere, as is evidenced by talking to many female colleagues of all ages and years of experience that continue to struggle with a lack of opportunity and support.

So Now What?

At annual conference, a milestone occurred not long ago. One of my young female mentees was ordained alongside an ordination class of only women. It was the first class in our conference of all women to be ordained. A female bishop, female clergy mentors, and female ordinands. I found at one point I had tears in my eyes, not because I don't deeply appreciate my male colleagues, but because it was a bellwether moment for The United Methodist Church. Seminaries continue to graduate classes that have a larger representation of women than men. Numbers of clergywomen continue to swell in most annual and central conferences in our connection, and we stand at a point where, without our female leadership, thousands of pulpits around the world would be empty. The Body of Christ cannot survive without the gifts women now bring to the modern Christian church.

Few people thought this day would ever come.

And this trend isn't changing or reversing course anytime soon.

A clergywoman friend of mine told the story of her night of being "seated" at a new appointment and when she was presented, the Pastor-Parish Relations Committee refused to receive her. So, the district superintendent calmly asked, "If you are not open to this pastor, I have two other very gifted pastors, who also just happen to be female, for you to receive. But these are your options, so I suggest you make a wise, Spirit-directed choice."

Perhaps, in the days ahead, churches who remain resistant or downright refuse to receive a woman in leadership will, too, have a choice to make. It will be imperative that our lay leadership as well as our superintendents continue to challenge these congregations to broaden their biblical understanding of God's call upon the lives of women. As the table is cleared for more to join in, perhaps we will all be encouraged to honor the Spirit's work in itinerancy, and in every human heart that is called to serve God's purposes—male and female alike.

What Can We Do Today?

I've encountered many churches and individuals that are aware of the unique challenges and opportunities that continue to face women, many exhibiting a genuine desire to be a part of the solution, rather than the problem. However, often these same individuals and churches get caught in a narrative of, "This struggle is just bigger than any of us. There's no way we, on a small scale, can truly make lasting change."

I would like to suggest that you and I—each and every one of us—truly can.

Keeping Women in the Forefront

These are some key considerations each of our United Methodist congregations must continue to ask to keep women in the forefront:

- **Encourage your pastor to place laywomen and men in preparatory leadership.** Even from the youngest ages, give women particularly a chance to lead beyond token positions that have very little influence or opportunity to contribute. So many times, clergy and laity learn a more excellent way of leadership by doing. Keep the wisdom of other worldwide organizations in mind and on the heart when raising up leadership—when only 50 percent of the population (of your church) has a voice in the vision and mission of your congregation, you are missing a vital perspective that must be heard.
- **Do not be surprised when a young woman comes to say she feels called to ministry.** Do you create a culture of call that encourages both young women and men to consider that a life of vocational ministry could be meant for them? If you haven't already, have conversations with your pastor, church leadership, youth and children's ministry staff, and/or volunteers to make it a priority to create a culture of call in your church to raise both young women and men. Expect and seek for that call to come forth for the sake of God's church.

- **Be mindful of boundary issues.** If a pastor or layperson expresses concerns about sexual harassment or unwanted actions involving staff, parishioners, or others connected to the church, take the concerns seriously. Most clergywomen will probably encounter such situations at some point. Make sure that church leadership has been trained to recognize instances of harassment and sexism.

Practical Solutions for the Congregation

Here are some practical solutions if you are receiving a new pastor who is female or if you already are being pastored by a clergywoman.[11]

- **When you do receive a pastor who is female, treat her as your pastor first.** Her gender should not be the lead in conversations. Talk about her as you would a new male pastor. Use the proper title that communicates you recognize the authority she holds in your church and community, or ask what she would like to be called. Avoid using affectionate terms and resist gender-specific language such as "woman pastor" or "lady pastor." When considering your pastor's compensation, do not lower it because of gender or assumptions that the pastor may have benefits coverage or income from her spouse.
- **Avoid stereotyping and assumptions.** Though this may be a major shift for your congregation, much more will likely be the same than will become different. Keep the expectations for your pastor the same as they have always been and trust that she will bring her own unique

ministry gifts to the position. Don't assume she will be good with children, but not finance. Don't expect her to bring treats for meetings or host a gathering at her home. Women and men both often have family responsibilities, and the congregation must trust that their pastor will navigate the expectations of congregation and home well and on their own terms. When questions or comments arise about the pastor's personal life, relationships, family plans, or body, the question to remember is: "Would you honestly ask (say, criticize) this if the pastor were a man? If not, drop it."

- **Encourage her to teach about perspectives on women in ministry.** When receiving a female pastor, no matter what part of the connection one resides in, there are still often some levels of questioning, curiosity, and resistance that often (not always) are healed through time spent together in transparent conversation and study. Offering an invitation for teaching about biblical perspectives will give her a platform to dispel biblical misunderstandings that some in your congregation may hold, whether expressed or not. One of the best gifts you can offer as a lay leader is staying engaged in her ministry and paying attention. Become acquainted with her leadership and witness the fruit of God's work through her as a spiritual leader.

Communion

God is opening the very real possibility of renewed hope within a wounded church—our God "who is able to do far beyond all that we could ask or imagine by his power at work within us" (Ephesians 3:20). God is continuing to raise up people of all kinds from accepting the crumbs from the Communion Table to powerfully presiding and taking their place at the Table to lead and serve for the sake of a hurting world. I have seen and experienced this in my own congregation, who, only two years ago, received me as their first clergywoman in their seventy-year history. God's Spirit is opening new pathways for congregations and communities to hold space for women especially to faithfully stand, take our place, and live out our call.

Whenever we witness the opportunity and flourishing of one oppressed group finally coming to fulfillment, we find that everyone, in one way or another, rises.

We rise together to a higher perspective of how God has the surprising capacity to work through others, and by virtue of that, work also through each of us.

We rise together to cast out the evils of our hatred, past discrimination, and complicity to embrace a new future filled with diverse relationships and endless possibilities.

We rise together to respect all people as blessed children of God, and see the unjust ways we are oppressing others that still have a voice on the margins.

We rise together to speak our truth, tell our stories, and call up the voices and gifts of those that still remain silenced.

Women's leadership is not an "issue"—just as race is not an "issue" and human sexuality is not an "issue." To speak of women's leadership is to speak of a commitment to people whom God has placed among us to assist in bringing the reign of God closer to our reality. Jesus reminds us, "'Look, here it is!' or 'There!' for behold, the kingdom of God is in the midst of you" (Luke 17:20-21 ESV). May we never miss the ways to respond to the reign of God emerging all around us. This is not just a responsibility for those in the center of privilege to hold, but a mission for everyone.

Communion Prayer

God of women and men,

Christ of the table at which we gather and share your bounty,

Spirit who blows to convict, challenge, comfort, and inspire,

It is you who invites us all from the city streets and the darkest alleyways and even the highest places of power to come, take a seat, and have our fill. Have mercy on us when we don't freely respond to your invitation to commune with all sisters and brothers you have called to leadership in your church. If we have made our excuses out of fear, comfort us; out of pride, deliver us; out of a lack of empathy for the struggle of others, challenge us; and if out of hatred, unforgiveness or disdain for another, heal us, O God. You are our God of the abundant table spread, help us to always believe that there is enough for everyone. Give us your eyes to see and ears to hear so we may rejoice for that which you rejoice, and weep for that which you weep. Above all, humble us to see the value and gifts in every person you call to Christian service. Break open and shatter the molds that have hardened around what effective leadership is, and help us, today and always, discover together the glorious future of what can be. In the name of God, our grace-filled Host. Amen.

Chapter Six

OUR MISSION

Juan Huertas

The church would betray its own love for God and its fidelity to the gospel if it stopped being . . . a defender of the rights of the poor . . . a humanizer of every legitimate struggle to achieve a more just society . . . that prepares the way for the true reign of God in history.

—Oscár Romero

I grew up in a parsonage; the rhythms of pastoral life have been integral to my formation since I was about five. The church of my childhood was the Latin American church. Vibrant worship, eating together, and a deep commitment to the neighborhood (and to neighbors) were part of what it meant to be church.

One of the most formative events in my life happened when I was about seven years old. My dad (who was the church's pastor) gave me a grocery bag and told me to fill it up with some canned goods. He did the same. We got in the car and as we got closer to our destination he told me that this person from our church that we were going to visit was going through a hard time financially. We were going to knock on their door, greet, give the bags, and pray. We were then going to come back home and never speak of what we did, because we would not want to embarrass the family. Why did we do that? Because that's what the church does!

From the moment I could read, I was immersed in the story of faith found in Scripture. I was fascinated by the story of Jesus, the miracles, the healing, the conversations that Jesus had with unlikely people. All of it began to shape an understanding of what it meant to do what Jesus does and to see that doing is what it means to be in mission.

Mission=Discipleship

In this chapter we'll struggle together about what it means for mission to be a mark of hope. As I shared in the chapter on justice, as the Spanish language makes clear, hope is a state of being, the state of waiting, I argue that our understanding of mission is only a mark of hope if we begin to see it beyond the confines of our own community. Mission is a mark of hope only if we give it flesh and make it evident among the people with whom we live, work, and play. A mission is an assignment that we are sent to, empowered for, to be dispatched and released for. A mission is the reason for why a group or an individual exists, their reason for being. Mission is active, empowering, and generative.

Jesus reminded us why he came:

- "He came as a witness to testify concerning the light, so that through him everyone would believe in the light" (John 1:7).

- "Jesus replied, 'If God were your Father, you would love me, for I came from God. Here I am. I haven't come on my own. God sent me'" (John 8:42 NRSV).
- "I came so that they could have life—indeed, so that they could live life to the fullest" (John 10:10b).
- "So you are a king?" Pilate said. Jesus answered, "You say that I am a king. I was born and came into the world for this reason: to testify to the truth. Whoever accepts the truth listens to my voice" (John 18:37).

In our baptism we make a claim to make Christ our Lord and to "remain *faithful members* of Christ's holy church and serve as Christ's *representatives* in the world."[1] Being Christ's representatives means that our mission, our calling, our reason for being are rooted in being like Christ, in representing the ministry of Jesus.

> *He called for the Twelve and sent them out in pairs. He gave them authority over unclean spirits. He instructed them to take nothing for the journey except a walking stick—no bread, no bags, and no money in their belts. He told them to wear sandals but not to put on two shirts. He said, "Whatever house you enter, remain there until you leave that place. If a place doesn't welcome you or listen to you, as you leave, shake the dust off your feet as a witness against them." So they went out and proclaimed that people should change their hearts and lives. They cast out many demons, and they anointed many sick people with olive oil and healed them.*
>
> *(Mark 6:7-13)*

Mission as a mark of hope is rooted in our commitment to discipleship. Our discipleship calls us and empowers us to use

God's given gifts for the building up of the body called the church (Ephesians 4:12) so that that the body can be Christ in the world, healing, restoring, freeing, welcoming, and forgiving (e.g., Matthew 25, Matthew 11:2-6, Mark 6:7-13, Mark 8:34-38, Luke 4:18, Luke 24:46-49, John 20:19-23). This commitment requires formation, training, practice in the way of Jesus. It requires that we, like the disciples of long ago, are sent two by two into our communities to see God's mission in action.

Our congregations at their best are incubators of growth in love, the way of Jesus, and missional imagination. We do this by telling and retelling the story of God's work in the world, gathering around tables in our communities and in the church, and in prayer individually and in community. These practices push us beyond ourselves into the messiness of life in community with our neighbors, coworkers, friends, and foes.

Our Present Reality

For the last twelve years as a pastor I have been to countless meetings where we discussed how to be in mission. We've done surveys, assessments, reports, interviews, and evaluations. In Louisiana we have also done countless hours of recovery work. In spite of our efforts and our long history in some communities I look around and realize that the key systemic hungers, diseases, deaths, and demon possessions are still present, sometimes even more actively present, even when there's a congregation in the community. It makes me ask the question: Has Jesus been here?

In our current denominational divisions we have another example of what I see as our lack of mission. We continue to fight with one another, continue to argue intellectual positions, and deny the full humanity of people that are unlike us. Our arguments, questioning of one another's faith, and treatment of each other, not like siblings but like enemies, makes it evident that we will not be fruitful until the Holy Spirit missions us. Imagine if we put half of the energies that we have spent arguing with one another about LGBTQ issues in efforts to restore, redeem, and renew?

I recognize that it is difficult to get over our particular positions because we are living in times of fast change. Anxiety, fear, and suspicion permeate our public life. We are becoming more segregated by affinities and this is making it difficult for us to see mission beyond that which makes us feel good about ourselves. Mission should be alongside the other, the different, the one that we do not understand, the one that even though an enemy is loved by God! In a recent conversation, I asked the question: Is this missional initiative about making Jesus known or about giving a missional opportunity for us to feel happy about ourselves? Our congregational insularity is keeping us from the world-transforming call of Jesus at a time when good news is sorely needed.

Although these are frustrating and disappointing times in the life of the church, I do know that God is using us to be bearers of God's mission. My hope is that this conversation we are having opens our eyes to what God is already doing around us. Often I gather our leaders and walk them around our campus, and as we walk I tell stories of what I see God doing. At other times I invite them to drive from their neighborhood to the church with an open mind and heart so that they might see their neighbors in new ways. Some years ago when I served a congregation in the middle of a neighborhood, we walked the neighborhood together, we prayed, but we also met our neighbors.

I invite you as you read to remind yourself that you are a sent one, one who belongs to a sent body, you are one who has encountered Jesus, who helps others do the same, while at the same time being one who is continually seeking to meet Jesus again, along the way, as you live life as a member of the body called the church. You are also one who in sharing your stories of encounter can inspire your baptized community to live in a sent way, anointed way, missional way. You become a catalyst for your congregation to live into its unique call where you are, among those whom God has placed you, at this pivotal time in our communities and in our world.

We are where we are for a reason.

Mission as Identity

The idea of the missional church emerged in the late '90s as a response to the decline of the North American church. I can remember hearing about it for the first time in the early 2000s as a "new thing" happening around us. This conversation came in recognition that the church needed to be reformed, that we needed to recover our apostolic witness of the first centuries of the church, that we needed to recover our identity. The conversation was happening at a time when I was considering walking away from the Christian church because it didn't seem the church was making a difference in our world. Alan Hirsh, pastor, theologian, and missional church advocate defines missional church as:

> [A] community of God's people that defines itself, and organizes its life around, its real purpose of being an agent of God's mission to the world. In other words, the church's true and authentic organizing principle is mission. When the church is in mission, it is the true church. The church itself is not only a product of that mission but is obligated

and destined to extend it by whatever means possible. The mission of God flows directly through every believer and every community of faith that adheres to Jesus. To obstruct this is to block God's purposes in and through his people.[2]

In United Methodism the idea of a church for God's mission should not be a surprise. Our movement was founded on responding to the needs of neighbor as a key practice for life in God. As our founder John Wesley reminds us:

> Secondly, all works of mercy, whether they relate to the bodies or souls of men; such as feeding the hungry, clothing the naked, entertaining the stranger, visiting those that are in prison, or sick, or variously afflicted . . . or contribute in any manner to the saving of souls from death. This is the repentance, and these the fruits meet for repentance, which are necessary to full sanctification. This is the way wherein God hath appointed his children to wait for complete salvation.[3]

Indeed many of our congregations are deeply involved in the work of helping neighbor, providing for the least of these, and relief and recovery ministry. I am sure that if you take a short walk on your church campus you will find flyers, buckets for food collection, and maybe even a missions committee meeting in the church's calendar. So what are some ways that we can reclaim this identity in our local context? How do we begin to rethink our understanding of the purpose and reason for being a congregation?

1. Answer the Call of the Community

In the summer of 2011 I found myself in the small dining hall of our Children's Center. For forty years St. John's United

Methodist Church had provided a space for children to receive an early childhood education and to be cared for in love. In the early days it was an important mission of the congregation. Some of the older members told stories of their own children attending and their congregation seeing this ministry as one of the reasons why they were there at the corner of Renee and Highland Road.

It was around 4:30 in the afternoon and I was in the dining hall because I had just received a call that our forty-year mission to our neighbors would have to close. The reasons were related to state requirements, shifting congregational priorities, and leadership struggles. It seemed like our mission was over.

I stood in the midst of the space and fought back tears as I prayed. I wondered what God was doing, what we could learn, and what might emerge out of this difficult situation?

Four months later one of our lay leaders entered my office and shared a vision that she believed was from God. At the time I wondered if this vision was for our congregation or for her, a faithful follower of Jesus. She was indeed a prophetic voice among us, she heard God call her to "feed my sheep" (John 21:17b).

Six years later the Shepherd's Market feeds over four hundred families a month. A "client choice" food pantry located in the old dining hall of the Children's Center, it seeks to feed people's body, mind, and spirit. The market provides a space where volunteers come alongside community members in need to make relationships, share stories, and eat together. On pantry day it is not unusual to see people praying for each other, playing with the kids, and learning about job opportunities.

See, our mission as a church was not over when the Children's Center closed. We were still called to be agents of good news, of healing, wholeness, and new life. What had ended was the way we lived out that call. The closure forced us to look around, listen to God and to our neighbors, and respond like Jesus would.

2. Take Action

Too often we become discouraged and stuck when long-term ministries end or no longer seem to be hope-filled places. Maybe our neighborhoods are changing, attendance patterns are no longer the same, and/or there is a lack of energy around us. We might find that the people we encounter do not want what we want for a church, are not like us, and might even live lives that are not how we would live our lives. The good news of Jesus calls us and has equipped us as the baptized to be the people for such times, for in the midst of chaos, confusion, and change, God comes to bring wholeness, healing, and new life. God brings salvation.

I know that St. John's UMC is not alone. There are many congregations across our connection that are seeing new possibilities emerge. These congregations are connecting to their neighbors and to God, finding new and renewed life as they answer the call of God's mission. In order to faithfully take action, congregations must practice prayer, conversation, and discernment as we seek to be mission-centered communities.

Action begins with us as we talk to our fellow baptized and prayerfully pay attention to what is emerging. We must help each other remember that the Spirit of God has set us apart for God's mission and God will guide us if we are open and willing to participate.

3. Overcome Mission Barriers

Often when we begin to take action, we also begin to find barriers among us. They can be barriers within ourselves as questions arise about how the church is taking care of us. We have fueled a model of congregational life that has centered around being cared for, so it is not surprising that this is often a huge barrier to missional identity. No wonder we become insular when we hear that the church is dying.

As I think about how to help my congregation to be hopeful so that we can be fruitful (and faithful), I keep identifying a series of attitudes, practices, and ways of thinking that I believe create barriers to our living into the call of Jesus and the many ways that keep our congregations from seeing their gifts and abilities to be like Jesus in their communities.

Do we recognize that in many ways we have lost our mission, our reason for being? I think that we have lost our way because we have spent too much time worried about our past, about what is most comfortable, and about our current situation individually and as a community. We have lost our way because we have believed that the church exists for our benefit as individuals.

Our current situation as the church reminds me of the story of the transfiguration:

> *Six days later Jesus took Peter, James, and John his brother, and brought them to the top of a very high mountain. He was transformed in front of them. His face shone like the sun, and his clothes became as white as light.*
>
> *Moses and Elijah appeared to them, talking with Jesus. Peter reacted to all of this by saying to Jesus, "Lord, it's good that we're here. If you want, I'll make three shrines: one for you, one for Moses, and one for Elijah."*
>
> *(Matthew 17:1-4)*

4. Find Your Identity

Like Peter, James, and John we build more shrines for our comfort, enjoyment, and personal connection to Jesus. Often our motives are good, we want to experience the awe for ourselves, we want to be with those like us, we do not want to risk going back down the mountain. Yet Jesus calls us to come down the mountain for it is in the valley that we are needed as disciples. It is there that we get to exercise the power given to us on the mountain. It is in the valley, in the every day of life that we make Jesus known, that our identity as the church is made witnessed.

In order to reclaim our identity we must be willing to ask the difficult questions:

- What does it mean for us to be the body of Christ? The community of those who have encountered Christ? The people who have experienced the Christ's salvation (healing, wholeness, peace, restoration, and redemption)?
- Do we believe that our congregation more than any other in our community is ready to be the kind of community that Jesus instituted?
- How do we live into that call where we live, work, and play?

One of my favorite movies is *The Shawshank Redemption*, the story of an innocent man, Andy Dufresne, who is sent to the penitentiary to serve a life sentence for murdering his wife. One day as he marked another week in prison, a piece fell off of the wall. At that moment he went from despair to hope as he found his mission inside the penitentiary. From that moment his whole life became focused on digging a tunnel. He did not know where it would lead or if it would work. All Andy knew was that his mission in the end would be his salvation.

5. Share Hope; an Invitation

Congregations that are living mission as a mark of hope realize that our moments of awe and wonder are meant to be shared. These moments must serve to push us back down the mountain, for it is down there that the Holy Spirit is preparing not only the way for our growth in grace but also for our transformation, our engagement and participation in God's mission in the world. No wonder God gets Peter, James, and John's attention and reminds them to listen. As soon as they go down the mountain they are given the opportunity to live into their call, to fulfill their mission.

People around us are in need of healing, wholeness, and new life. They are also in need to be freed, like we have been, from all the things that keep us bound. Are we going to have the faith to live into God's mission?

Unfortunately our faith has become a passive one. The most pious among us continue to attend worship (go to church) and attempt to be a good person. We desire more but are unaware of what that means or how to make that a reality. Many other things call our name, capturing our attention and imagination. Those other things feed our passivity, lulling us into thinking that our faith is about a set of beliefs instead of a call to be part of a mission—God's mission in the world.

Some among us feel the tug for more, for some activity. I think this is why mission as activity emerges as primary initiative in many of our churches. We know that there must be more, and we want to feel good about our church and ourselves. So, we decide that activity is the way to go. We feed hungry people, we paint houses, we build ramps, and we give money for others to do those things. All of these activities are good, but this is not the type of mission that develops and fuels hope.

I know that it is hard to believe that we could be agents of God's mission. We read of the healing, exorcisms, resuscitations, liberation, inclusion, and sacrifice that characterize God's mission and we can easily dismiss it, ignore it, and/or think that it is something to merely inspire us to be good people. Yet it is in our living of this mission that our own salvation is worked out, our own identity clarified, and our reason for being God's people—the church—fulfilled.

Hopeful congregations constantly remind each other that what is impossible for us becomes possible with God. By the power of the Holy Spirit, the baptized community has been given all it needs to live into its mission, and in doing so continues to become a more powerful mark of hope.

Missional Church—Missionary Body

Living into God's mission requires formation. None of us are able to live into our call as God's people without consistent practices that help us grow in love of God and neighbor. We also know that worship is one of those practices, but we must realize that it is only one and by itself it is unable to shape a missional imagination.

In my own life I've struggled to keep myself focused. Pastors are no less easily distracted with the work of the church. We also struggle with choosing comfortable and familiar over difficult and risky. We also would rather lead in ways that are safe and easy to control.

This past summer after twelve years of ministry I took a six-week sabbatical. For those six weeks I was relieved of my duties as pastor. At first I was anxious about being away, about not being part of the church's life, but most of all I was afraid of losing control. As

I began my time away I quickly felt a sense of relief, a freedom, and a growing creativity and openness.

The second week of my sabbatical I traveled to St. John's Abbey in Collegeville, Minnesota. I had been to St. John's Abbey fifteen years before as a fellow with the Fund for Theological Exploration. Since that time I had wanted to return and spend some time there reflecting, thinking, and writing. I was thankful to have the opportunity to get away and hear God's voice in the silence.

The second day I went out for a long walk in the woods. The weather was beautiful and in the silence I could hear the birds, the insects, the wind over the lake, and I could also hear God. As I walked it quickly became apparent that God was calling me to let go. The word that kept surfacing in my mind was the word *surrender*. Surrender is not a word that I like to think about because as a pastor I had spent so much energy trying to control. The more that I walked, the more that I let go, and the more that hope began to emerge—hope for my walk with God, hope for the people I pastored, and hope for our unique call in our community.

Congregations that are hopeful are learning to practice surrender as they work toward God's mission by giving of themselves to the power of the Holy Spirit, a Spirit who then calls them and sends them to serve. This means letting go of anything that might keep us from living fully into God's way of life. Like the rich young ruler in the Mark's Gospel, selling all that we have (all that controls us) and following Jesus.

> *Jesus looked at him carefully and loved him. He said, "You are lacking one thing. Go, sell what you own, and give the money to the poor. Then you will have treasure in heaven. And come, follow me." But the man was dismayed at this statement*

and went away saddened, because he had many
possessions.

(Mark 10:21-22)

It is easier to paint, build stuff, and collect supplies, all good things that I believe strengthen our distraction. It is harder to allow God to make us "one with Christ, one with each other, and one in ministry to all the world."

Once we surrender there is no telling what we might hear God asking of us. The gifts and graces given to us by the Holy Spirit become activated for service in God's restorative mission in and for the world. Together as the community of the baptized, we are diverse, we are multifaceted, we are abundantly gifted to make the kingdom of God known.

Learning to surrender to God's mission requires prayer, reflection on Scripture, and community in and through Holy Communion. John Wesley wrote:

> The chief of these means are prayer, whether in secret or with the great congregation; searching the Scriptures (which implies reading, hearing, and meditating thereon) and receiving the Lord's Supper, eating bread and drinking wine in remembrance of him; and these we believe to be ordained of God as the ordinary channels of conveying his grace to the souls of men.[4]

In our congregation we have realized that we need to put in more time helping our people learn how to pray. Like Jesus did with his disciples, we must do. This training in prayer must include our private prayer that aligns our will to God, as well as our public prayer including confession, praise, thanksgiving, and supplication. As we pray individually, with small groups of believers, and as God's people in worship, we grow into what it means to participate in making God's will done "on earth as it's done in heaven."

I cannot emphasize enough how important it is for all followers of Jesus to become immersed in the story of Jesus as found in the Gospels. The more we immerse ourselves in the story of Jesus, the more able we will become like him in doing God's mission in the world because we will know what it looks like. Immersing ourselves in the story of Jesus in the Gospels also guides our reading of the rest of God's story in the Bible, which deepens our own understanding and action toward God's mission in the world.

Jesus promised us that he would be known in the breaking of the bread. The book of Acts tells us that "the Lord added to their number" (Acts 2:47 NRSV) those who were being saved as the community practiced the breaking of the bread. In my own pastoral practice I have seen again and again the power of Holy Communion in making us "one with Christ, one with each other, and one in ministry to all the world." Practicing Holy Communion weekly reminds us of our call, of being about God's mission. It also empowers us by the Holy Spirit and sends us into the world prepared to be God's people, doing what God does.

I am amazed at the power of gathering around God's Table. I am humbled each time as I see people coming forth for a crumb of bread and a sip from the cup. I am in awe as I see people have God moments, moments of connection, clarity, and community. I am inspired as I see little hands eager and frail hands expectant. The more we gather around the Table, the more faithful we become at God's mission and the more we recognize how deeply connected we are to one another. Like the first disciples we gather as a diverse community: tax collector and zealot, competing fishermen, the one who speaks before thinking and the one who thinks and hardly speaks, the beloved disciple, and the traitor. All together, all different, all beloved.

Think about your own practices of prayer, Scripture, and Holy Communion. How do you live into those in your own community? How are they shaping your missional imagination?

Shaping our people into a missional imagination means shaping them as disciples of Jesus. Churches that are *hope-full* are finding ways to help their people become more faithful disciples by reconnecting them to their identity as a baptized people, a people transformed for and by God's mission—a people whose ears have been shaped to answer God's call.

As I write this I find myself in McAllen, Texas. I am here to gather with other leaders across the South Central Jurisdiction of The United Methodist Church to dialogue, experience, and reflect about our ministry alongside Hispanic/Latinos in our context. We've heard key demographic information, some theological markers, and helpful wisdom about the Spanish language. As I look around I realize that most leaders gathered are white, male, and part of the leadership structure of their particular annual conferences. I also notice much curiosity, excitement, and desire to reach out in ways that are true to the gospel and to the cultural context.

As we took a tour of El Valle, "the valley," we began to be awakened. Earlier that morning Bishop Cynthia Harvey had encouraged us to be open to encounter the serendipitous ways that we stumble upon another, the surprising ways that we see Jesus around us, and the Spanish language around us.

Until my sabbatical last summer I was not aware of how much I missed being immersed in my native language. Something familiar, warm, and comfortable made my senses more sensitive to the sights, sounds, and smells that I was experiencing. Hearing my language spoken by United Methodists made my connection to this denomination I love even stronger.

Seeing walls, border patrol agents, and barbwire brought sadness, curiosity, and many questions. In some ways I am still processing the experience, but I kept on thinking about the ways that my United Methodist brothers and sisters were doing ministry in the midst of all of this. They were showing up at the border, in detention centers, and in the colonias.[5] I began to wonder how I would respond in the midst of so many missional needs.

It was later that evening that my questions began to be answered. We visited a house church in Los Naranjos (The Oranges) and I saw the missional impetus in action. A small group of people gathered, worshiped on the back porch of a humble wood dwelling, then ate together. They praised, prayed, and played. People of all ages gathered, shared stories, and spoke of the amazing things that God was doing in their life. Hearing them I was touched, inspired, and convicted.

See, they were living the way of Jesus in the most natural way. They were gathering, eating together, and paying attention to their neighbors. They were making room for people where they were. It was not fancy (it was outside and very hot), it was not polished, but it was Spirit filled! They found a way to live the way of Jesus, to live their baptism, to live their calling, where they were.

It dawned on me that as we answer our unique call together we become a potent force for wholeness, healing, and reconciliation in the world. Now instead of doing to help, we do to be; instead of doing good things, we do transformative things; instead of feeling good about ourselves, we feel good about the other. Little by little, being by being, we become active participants, we become God-doers, salvation facilitators for the life of the world. With each movement we make our mission becomes another mark of hope in a hopeless world.

What You Can Do Today

It is my prayer that this chapter is not another missional call that leaves us discouraged, frustrated, and hopeless. My desire is that this chapter awakens your missional imagination, creativity, and your baptism. Gather your people, eat together, sing a song, and then:

- Do an inventory of your community, your congregation, and your resources. Go outside, walk the neighborhood, take a shuttle tour and ask:
  o What are we passionate about?
  o What is God doing around us?
  o How have we been uniquely gifted by the Holy Spirit to bring good news in this place at this time?

- Think about the conversations that your people are having in administrative meetings, in your Sunday school class, or around the coffeepot:
  o What do those conversations have in common?
  o What themes keep emerging?
  o What is the tone and tenor of the conversations?
  o How often is the phrase *God's mission, way of Jesus*, or *make disciples* at the center of the conversations?

- Practice Confession and Pardon together:
  o Have we become self-centered?
  o Have we settled for less than a life of deepening relationship with God and neighbor?
  o How have we chosen comfort with our own sin, spiritual immaturity, and worldly desires over the struggle and freedom that is life with God?

o Do we recognize that our life together, our life worship, study, fellowship, and service is about growing more deeply in love of God, self, and neighbor, not about friendship, socialization, or networking?

o Have we made our encounter with Jesus our own private experience instead of an experience that moves us beyond ourselves and connects us with others?

Communion

When we gather around the Table, many of our churches remind us of whose Table we gather around. Often the pastor says something like: "This is not my table, or this congregation's table, this is the Lord's Table and all are invited."

As you gather for Holy Communion, who is the "all" that are invited? Is it really all? Who is missing, how does your Table fellowship reflect the neighborhood that you live in, the city that you are located at, and the vision of Jesus in the Gospels?

As you eat and drink at your next time around the Table, I invite you to pray. Pray that you and the people around you can become the body of Christ. Pray that your community can become "one with Christ, one with each other, and one in ministry to all the world." Pray that in taking this bread and drinking this cup all of you might be transformed into Christ.

Now imagine yourself doing what Jesus does: healing, welcoming, asking questions of strangers, and inviting himself to dinner. Now confess that often you fail at doing what Jesus does and being who Jesus is. Now imagine, the world that Jesus dreamed about, the ministry that Jesus made possible, the mission that Jesus called all of us to, and the meal that Jesus gave us so that we could live into that mission—that call.

Communion Prayer

Bread broken, cup shared, now we are ready.
Bread broken, cup shared, now we remember.
Bread broken, cup shared, now we know what love looks like,
our eyes are open, our spirit's willing,
now we are ready to make the reign of God visible,
still broken, still imperfect,
yet visible, not because we are perfect
but because bread and wine have given us,
all of us, the body of Christ given what it needs.
Hope emerging as we are empowered to do what Jesus has done,
to be a missional people, to be the body of Christ for the life of the world!
Amen.

NOTES

Chapter One

1. Don Bryant, "How Do I Get There," on *Don't Give Up on Love* album, Fat Possum Records, 2017.
2. From audiotape of Thomas Merton's final talk as novice master on August 20, 1965; quoted in Marcus Borg, *The Heart of Christianity* (San Francisco: Harper San Francisco, 2003), 155.

Chapter Two

1. Josh Kinney, "Entrepreneurship Summit Re-Imagines Mission," The United Methodist Church of Greater New Jersey, July 5, 2016, https://www.gnjumc.org/news /entrepreneurship-summit-re-imagines-mission/.
2. David W. Scott, "Social Entrepreneurship in the Cote d'Ivoire UMW," UM & Global, December 16, 2014, http://www .umglobal.org/2014/12/social-entrepreneurship-in-cote -divoire.html.

3. Joe Iovino, "Methodist history: Controversy, Communion, & Welch's Grape Juice," United Methodist Communications, June 28, 2016, http://www.umc.org/who-we-are/methodist -history-controversy-communion-and-welchs-grape-juice.

4. Kenneth Carder, "Fresh Expressions, United Methodism and 'Saving the Institution,'" The Florida Conference of The United Methodist Church blog, November 2, 2015, https:// www.flumc.org/blogdetail/fresh-expressions-united -methodism-and-saving-the-institution-2662779.

5. Gil Rendle, "The Legacy Conversation: Helping a Congregation Die with Dignity," *Circuit Rider*, Feb/Mar /April 2011, http://www.ministrymatters.com/all/entry/716 /the-legacy-conversation-helping-a-congregation-die-with -dignity.

6. Scott, "Social Entrepreneurship in the Cote d'Ivoire UMW."

7. Mike Baughman, "The Wetlands Where Church and Social Ventures Meet," Faith & Leadership, November 4, 2013, https://www.faithandleadership.com/mike-baughman -wetlands-where-church-and-social-ventures-meet.

8. W. Craig Gilliam, *Where Angels Dare to Dance: Anxiety & Conflict in Congregational Life* (Washington, DC: JustPeace, 2013), 19.

Chapter Three

1. Miguel A. de la Torre, *Doing Christian Ethics from the Margins* (Maryknoll, NY: Orbis Books, 2014), 8.

2. "Baptismal Covenant I," *The United Methodist Hymnal* (Nashville: The United Methodist Publishing House, 1989), 34.

3. Mary McClintock Fulkerson and Marcia W. Mount Shoop, *A Body Broken, A Body Betrayed: Race, Memory, and Eucharist in White-Dominant Churches* (Eugene, OR: Cascade Books, 2015), 55.

Chapter Four

1. See John Wesley, "Predestination Calmly Considered" (1752), ed. Paul Wesley Chilcote and Kenneth J. Collins, vol. 13 of *The Works of John Wesley: Doctrinal and Controversial Treatises II* (Nashville: Abingdon Press, 2013), 261–320.

Chapter Five

1. The General Commission on the Status and Role of Women in The United Methodist Church, "Equity, opportunity, a continuing challenge," *The Flyer* Winter/Spring 1992, http://www.gcsrw.org/Portals/13/PDFs/FlyerArchive/1992 /Flyer Volume XII, No. 4 Winter Spring 1992.pdf.
2. Jackie Campbell, "Female Clergy Celebrate, But Struggle Continues," Western Pennsylvania Annual Conference of The United Methodist Church, November 11, 2016, https://www.wpaumc.org/newsdetail/struggle-for-women -clergy-rights-continues-6662633
3. Tobin Grant, "Gender Pay Gap among Clergy Worse than National Average—A First Look at the New National Data," Religion News Service, January 12, 2016, http://religionnews .com/2016/01/12/gender-pay-gap-among-clergy-worse -than-national-average-a-first-look-at-the-new- national-data/.
4. Campbell, "Female Clergy Celebrate, But Struggle Continues."

5. Margaret S. Wiborg and Elizabeth J. Collier, "Chapter One: The Problem Emerging," *United Methodist ClergywomEn Retention Study* (Boston: Anna Howard Shaw Center, Boston University School of Theology, 1999), http://www.bu.edu/ shaw/publications/the-clergy-womens-retention-study/ united-methodist-clergywomen-retention-study/.

6. Hee An Choi and Jacqueline Beatrice Blue, "In and Out" in *United Methodist Clergywomen Retention Study II* (Boston: Anna Howard Shaw Center, Boston University School of Theology, 2013), http://www.bu.edu/shaw /publications/united-methodist-clergywomen -retention-study-ii-2/.

7. Anna Marie Valerio and Katina Sawyer, "The Men Who Mentor Women," *Harvard Business Review*, December 7, 2016, https://hbr.org/2016/12/the-men-who-mentor-women.

8. Marcus Noland, Tyler Moran, and Barbara Kotschwar, "Is General Diversity Profitable? Evidence from a Global Survey," Working Paper 16-3, February 2016, Peterson Institute for International Economics. Available at https://piie.com /publications/working-papers/gender-diversity-profitable -evidence-global-survey.

9. Carole Cotton Winn, phone conversation with author, October 2017.

10. W. Brad Johnson and David G. Smith, "Men Shouldn't Refuse to Be Alone with Female Colleagues," *Harvard Business Review*, May 5, 2017, https://hbr.org/2017/05 /men-shouldnt-refuse-to-be-alone-with-female-colleagues.

11. Some portions adapted from part of the To the Point series, "Suggestions for Churches with a Clergywoman," Lewis Center for Church Leadership at Wesley Theological Seminary, September 19, 2015,

https://www.churchleadership.com/to-the-point/to-the-point
-suggestions-for-churches-with-a-clergywoman/.

Chapter Six

1.   The Baptismal Covenant I, *The United Methodist Hymnal*, 34.
2.   Alan Hirsch, *The Forgotten Ways: Reactivating the Missional Church* (Grand Rapids: Brazos Press, 2006), 82.
3.   John Wesley, Sermon 43, "The Scripture Way of Salvation," *The Works of John Wesley: Sermons II 34–70*, vol. 2., ed. Albert C. Outler (Nashville: Abingdon Press, 1985), 166.
4.   John Wesley, Sermon 16, "The Means of Grace," *The Works of John Wesley: Sermons I 1–33*, ed. Albert C. Outler (Nashville: Abingdon Press, 1984), 381.
5.   Colonias are unincorporated communities on the border that often lack basic infrastructure and services.

Psalm 33

Psalm 119   " hope in your word(s)

Jeremiah 29:11

Lamentations 3

Romans 5: 4-5 , 8:18- , 15:4-7, 13
I Corinthians 15:19

CPSIA information can be obtained
at www.ICGtesting.com
Printed in the USA
LVOW03s0755280318

571384LV00002B/2/P

9 781501 859335